AF234636

THE
SWORD
IN THE
STONE

THE SWORD IN THE STONE

A FOUR-THOUSAND-YEAR-OLD MYSTERY

LINDA A. MALCOR &
JOHN MATTHEWS

AMBERLEY

First published 2026

Amberley Publishing
The Hill, Stroud
Gloucestershire, GL5 4EP

www.amberley-books.com

Copyright © Linda A. Malcor & John Matthews, 2026

The right of Linda A. Malcor & John Matthews to
be identified as the Authors of this work has been
asserted in accordance with the Copyright, Designs
and Patents Act 1988.

ISBN 978 1 3981 2851 4 (hardback)
ISBN 978 1 3981 2852 1 (ebook)

All rights reserved. No part of this book may be
reprinted or reproduced or utilised in any form
or by any electronic, mechanical or other means,
now known or hereafter invented, including
photocopying and recording, or in any information
storage or retrieval system, without the permission
in writing from the Publishers.

British Library Cataloguing in Publication Data.
A catalogue record for this book is available from
the British Library.

1 2 3 4 5 6 7 8 9 10

Typesetting by SJmagic DESIGN SERVICES, India.
Printed in the UK.

Appointed GPSR EU Representative:
Easy Access System Europe Oü, 16879218
Address: Mustamäe tee 50, 10621, Tallinn, Estonia
Contact Details: gpsr.requests@easproject.com,
+358 40 500 3575

CONTENTS

To Elizabeth Wayland Barber and Paul Barber,
For their inspiration

... after the manner of barbarians a naked sword is fixed in the ground and they reverently worship it as their god of war.

Ammianus Marcellinus, XXXL, 2, 23,

Rolfe, ed. 1939: 393

... there was seen in the churchyard, against the high altar, a great stone four square, like unto a marble stone; and in midst thereof was like an anvil of steel a foot on high, and therein stuck a fair sword naked by the point, and letters there were written in gold about the sword that said thus: – Whoso pulleth out this sword of this stone and anvil, is rightwise king born of all England.

Thomas Malory: *Le Morte d'Arthur*.

Matthews, ed. 2020: 9

ACKNOWLEDGEMENTS

We would like to acknowledge C. Scott Littleton who, prior to his passing in 2010, authored and co-authored many of the papers on which the following chapters are based. Additionally, our thanks go to Elizabeth Wayland Barber and Paul Barber, without whose work this book would not exist. We wish to thank John Colarusso for his collection and translation of the Caucasian Nart Sagas – his input has been invaluable. We also appreciate the input of Caitlín Matthews, who read and commented upon several drafts.

PREFACE

Most people know the episode of the Sword in the Stone from the Arthurian tradition. According to Sir Thomas Malory, writing in the fifteenth century and following texts from Continental Europe, the twelve-year-old Arthur pulled a sword from an anvil atop a stone in a churchyard, thereby proving his right to become king of all England.[1] Another strand of the Arthurian tradition tells of Arthur and his Twelve Knights, the first to sit at the Round Table. It has long been assumed that Arthur inherited these heroes from stories of Charlemagne and his Twelve Companions, who in turn inherited them from Jesus and his Twelve Disciples.[2] Some writers, however, have seen an astronomical interpretation of the Twelve Companions.[3] Although this interpretation has largely been seen as 'out in left field' by mainstream scholarship, C. Scott Littleton and Linda A. Malcor found a growing body of evidence that the presence of twelve figures associated with Arthur did indeed come from a story written in the stars. The tale from which the twelve derived probably had nothing to do with either Charlemagne or Jesus, but rather with one of the many different iterations of the Sword in the Stone.

Alexandre Micha, as well as Littleton and Malcor, dealt with the tale of the Sword in the Stone in its non-Christian context to some extent,[4] but it was not until Elizabeth Wayland Barber and Paul Barber's *When They Severed Earth from Sky* appeared[5] that several of the proverbial pieces fell into their respective places and Littleton and Malcor realised that the story was part of a far more extensive tradition that told of something much older than Christianity. Accordingly, they developed a hypothesis that around 2160 Before the Common Era (BCE) an imported cosmic event became connected to a story about a sacred sword being plunged into a pile of brush, or a tree, which emerged among the ancient steppe peoples, triggered by a precession of the celestial pole that caused the perceived position of 'north' to 'shift'. The term 'Northshift' refers to the fact that the observed position of north 'moves' through the signs of the Tropical Zodiac over time. Our thesis here is that the pole, which takes roughly 2,160 years to pass through each sign of the Zodiac, and about 25,920 years to complete the entire cycle, can be represented by the image of the Sword in the Stone as well as by other weapons thrust into the ground and various other surfaces.[6]

Littleton died in 2010, and the book was shelved for a number of years until John Matthews agreed to team with Malcor to finish the work. We began by collecting all the known variants of embedded weapons that resembled the story of the Sword in the Stone, plotting the stories by date of recording and the places where they were documented. We have organised the material according to the types of object into which the weapon was plunged, then examined their spread through time and location. We have matched oral variants to written ones as closely as we could, following this with the historical content for each tale. From there we have compared the stories to the evidence collected by the Barbers and charted the results.

The following pages contain the results of our study, detailing each of the tales, placing them in historical context, and, finally, demonstrating how they were spread from the steppes of ancient Eurasia to places as remote in time and place as Los Angeles, California and Japan. So here, at last, is a resumé of 4,000-year-old story written in the stars.

Linda A. Malcor (Corona Del Mar, CA)

John Matthews (Oxford, UK)

INTRODUCTION

On 4 September 1781, a ragtag party of twenty-two adults and an equal number of children, led by Felipe de Neve, the newly appointed governor of Alta California, set out from Mission San Gabriel Archangel to found a new *pueblo*. When the party reached a spot some 10 miles west of the mission, near a Tongva Native American village called Ya-nga, Governor de Neve drew his sword and thrust it into the ground, solemnly proclaiming the founding of El Pueblo de la Nuestra Señora la Reina de Los Angeles (The Town of Our Lady the Queen of the Angels, i.e. Los Angeles). Thus began the history of what is today the second-largest city in the United States.[1]

Some 1,400 years earlier, in the late fourth century of the Common Era (CE), the Roman historian Ammianus Marcellinus recorded a similar custom among the Alans, a warlike tribe of steppe nomads who had begun to bedevil the western frontier of the Roman Empire and who will loom large in the following pages. According to Ammianus, the Alans were wont 'to stick a naked sword in the earth and worship it as the god of war, the presiding deity of the regions over which they range'.[2] Centuries later the Crusaders, some of them descended from the Alans,[3] would practise a related custom, plunging their sword into the ground and using the hilt as a cross with which to worship Jesus Christ.

Of course, it is extremely doubtful that Felipe de Neve worshipped his embedded sword as a god of war or even as Jesus Christ. Indeed, like most Spanish officials of the era, he was certainly a devout Roman Catholic for whom the hilt of the sword could only represent the Cross of Christ. Yet his ritualistic plunging of a naked blade into the earth that became the Plaza, the heart of downtown Los Angeles, reflected a very ancient complex of religious beliefs. These beliefs and practices associated with sacred and/or magical swords, both embedded and subsequently withdrawn, are best known to modern audiences through the legend of how the future King Arthur demonstrated his right to rule by pulling a sword from an anvil atop a stone and later just a stone. In this book we will trace the origin and distribution of this complex of tales, from the south Russian steppes to much of Eurasia and beyond, during the last four millennia. We will also attempt to show how the deep-seated symbolism inherent in this story is rooted in an ancient understanding of an astronomical event.

While the best-known example of the story of the Sword in the Stone comes from the tales of King Arthur and his Knights of the Round Table, scholarship on this particular motif has been sparse and generally uninspiring,[4] usually mentioned in passing or in an encyclopaedia article. In *The New Arthurian Encyclopedia*, editor Norris J. Lacy remarks that Robert de Boron, who first included the image of the Sword in the Stone in a story about Arthur, explains that the sword stands for justice.[5] This could be a reference to the Roman power of *jus gladii* (the Power of the Sword), which gave an official the right to carry out the death sentence against someone, even if that person was a senator. For example, the phrase appears on the memorial inscription to the second-century Roman officer Lucius Artorius Castus, one of the candidates for the historical King Arthur.

The stone in Robert de Boron's image is said to represent Christ, which varies from the thinking among the Crusaders of his time that the sword represented the Cross of Christ. Robert makes no mention of what the anvil means. This detail was long forgotten by the people who told the medieval tale, though a smith's anvil being pulled out of the earth was preserved in the Nart Sagas of the Caucasus Mountains.

In Arthur's case, the withdrawal of the sword, sometimes said to have been arranged by Merlin, is where the literature concentrates the reader's attention, while in other stories, such as that of the medieval Italian knight Galgano, the act of plunging the sword into the stone is the focus (see chapter 4). Lacy devotes one sentence to Merlin repeating the event with Galahad, who had to prove he was the Grail Knight just as Arthur had to prove he was the rightful king of all England. Littleton and Malcor devoted a short chapter to the topic in their book *From Scythia to Camelot*, which became the seed from which the present book has grown. Generally, scholars have been focused on what the withdrawal or plunging of the sword means, rather than what the image is doing while the sword is actually embedded in the stone, anvil or whatever other solid surface is handy.

As mentioned above, the thirteenth-century Burgundian poet Robert de Boron was the first to introduce this story into the

Arthurian tradition in a work entitled *Merlin*, and from this manuscript – which offers an overtly Christian interpretation of the sword – it spread to two other thirteenth-/fourteenth-century prose redactions, the *Suite du Merlin* and the Merlin portion of the *Lancelot-Grail* cycle.[6] Geoffrey of Monmouth, who introduced the figure of Arthur to a wider public in his *Historia Regnum Britanniae* (1185 CE), did not include the tale, and it does not appear elsewhere in the pseudo-histories of the period. The Arthurian Romances *do* contain the tale as well as that of several other famous swords of this type, which feature in stories of Lancelot, Galahad and the quest for the Grail.

The embedded sword quickly loses any attempt at an overt Christian interpretation when attached to the Arthurian tradition, a factor generally ignored by most modern scholars. This may be, in part at least, because the story began much earlier and travelled through a great many cultures, particularly those of the Central Eurasian Culture Complex, before it became attached to the vast range of Arthurian literature and myth.

The oldest image of the Sword in the Stone is probably that of the Hittite sword god embedded in a rock relief in Yazılıkaya, Turkey, which dates to *c.* 1250 BCE (see chapter 1). The sword itself, as a weapon, was invented *c.* 2000 BCE somewhere north-east of Mesopotamia, most likely on the Eurasian steppes.[7] Many of the stories from this time and later – and in several cultures – tell of the sword being forged in the Underworld by a disabled Divine Smith and how it was returned to its place of origin upon the death of its owner, when it is placed in his grave with him, usually along with his horse and armour.[8] In the folktales of the Caucasus

Mountain region, the sword, horse and armour are placed in a cellar beneath a wooden house, an image that resembles the *kurgans* (tombs) of the steppe peoples. The same tales relate how the warrior's heir proves that he can wear his father's armour, wield his sword and ride his horse, which suggests that sometimes these belongings were passed down to a son rather than being buried permanently with the warrior (see chapter 5).[9]

The Iranians told the story from a different point of view, resulting in tales of a sword thrust into a bull. The Scythians worshipped a sword in an altar atop a pile of wood, while their Alan relatives plunged the sword into the earth. Other descendants of the Alans, the Circassians, told of an anvil being pulled out of or plunged into and pulled out of seven or nine layers of earth, while in the Nart Sagas of the steppe lands the weapon is a lance rather than a sword. The Greeks split the story into two parts, telling of a Minotaur or bull-man and a sword *under* a stone. In Germanic tales the sword was plunged into trees and may have reappeared as one of the warrior Beowulf's two swords. On the periphery of the tradition, the sword is found in the Far East in the tail of a dragon in Japan, and in the West it travels to the New World via Spanish Conquistadors through Yorubaland in Africa, where it is thrust into the ground during religious ceremonies.

Typically, the types of variants of the tale of the Sword in the Stone would be considered an example of parallel development among peoples who spoke Indo-European languages. However, there are two major problems with this: Yorubaland, with the distribution to the Americas via the slave trade, and Japan. Given this clue, we can turn to the pattern of distribution of a specific Mediterranean tale that developed via what folklorists term 'diffusion', the passing of a story from one people to another. This is the myth of the Kingship in Heaven, which includes, as we shall see, references which connect it to the equally ancient origins of the Sword in the Stone.

The 'Kingship in Heaven'

The 'Kingship in Heaven' is really a series of tales, relating to the creation of the cosmos, which eventually spread by diffusion from the Near East to points as far afield as Finland and China.[10] As such, it provides us with a model for the tale of the Sword in the Stone was transmitted and how it changed along the way.

If all we had were the Hittite, Greek and Caucasian variants of the Kingship theme it would be very difficult – perhaps impossible – to determine the story's origin, since the interaction among those cultures was so extensive.[11] This interaction, however, makes it more likely that it was via diffusion rather than parallel development that tales from Near Eastern mythology – particularly when those stories have to do with creation – travelled across such huge distances.[12]

The 'Kingship in Heaven' pattern covers three generations and deals with the violent succession of a series of kings within the same family who destroy each other.[13] These stories probably originated among a people known as the Hurrians, who flourished *c.* 2254–2218 BCE. Around this time the Zodiac was starting to take shape, but in this variant the constellations were more important than the pole's passage through them. The earliest account we have of the myth is from the Hittite archives at Boğazköy,[14] and the Hittites focused on the pole of the heavens rather than the Zodiac itself. From their successors the story diffused from the Near East to other cultures.

Here is a summary of the variants:

Table 1. The Kingship in Heaven[15]

Culture	In the Beginning... Libra	First Generation Virgo	Second Generation Leo	Third Generation Cancer
Hurrian/ Hittite	ALALU First Heavenly King Hurled Down	ANU Emasculated by being bitten	KUMARBI Tries to eat own children; driven out	TESHUB Weather God (Ullikummi as monster)
Babylonian	APSU/ TIAMAT First Heavenly Couple Killed/ Widowed	ANSHAR/ KISHAR (=sky/earth) EA? ANU Kills Apsu HAIN	KINGU Driven out EA (ENKI) Divides Tiamat's body into world AMAKANDO	MARDUK Kills Tiamat and Kingu's children; divides Tiamat's body into heaven and earth ENLIL God of Wind LAHAR (Tiamat as monster)
Greek	CHAOS Yawning Void	OURANOS/ GAIA (=sky/earth) Emasculated with sickle	KRONOS Eats own children; driven out	ZEUS Storm God (Typhon as monster)

In the Hittite version we learn that heaven is ruled over by Alalu, who holds sway for nine years. His son is Anu, whose name means 'Heaven'. At first Anu obeys his father, then he turns on him and throws him down into the dark earth. Nine years later Anu is himself deposed by his son, Kumarbi. When Anu struggles to regain his power, Kumarbi bites off his father's genitals and swallows them. Anu tells Kumarbi that in so doing he has swallowed the divine seed that will give birth to five gods, including the storm god Teshub and the goddess of the Tigris river. The text is damaged here but the assumption is that despite his efforts to end the pregnancy by spitting out his father's sperm, the engendered offspring of the presiding deity are indeed born. They usually become associated with the intercalary days (where a day or month was inserted in order to make the calendar year correspond to the solar year) as in our modern leap year.

Kumarbi next tries to consume his offspring, but when the fragmentary text resumes he has been overthrown and Teshub is reigning. Bemoaning his defeat, Kumarbi copulates with a stone and begets a monster made of diorite, an igneous rock made of an assortment of minerals that is difficult to carve, who is known as Ullikummi. This monstrous creature is implanted in the shoulder of the sea god Upelluri, and soon grows so tall he threatens the very heavens. A despairing Teshub asks his sister Ishtar to seduce the giant, but this fails as Ullikummi is both blind and deaf. With the giant advancing, the gods retreat to Kummiya, on the seaboard of Syria. There Kumarbi decides to consult Ea, the Sumerian god of the purifying waters, who originated from the even older Sumerian pantheon, and who in turn seeks advice of Upelluri, who appears not to have noticed that the giant Ullikummi is attached to him. Using an ancient cutting tool that had once helped create the universe, the sea god severs the connection with the stone giant, who loses his strength and is defeated. The text ends here, but the story clearly was carried around the ancient Near East until it arrived in Babylon.

There, according to the Babylonian *Enuma Elish* (*c.* 2000 BCE), the universe began in streams of unformed water. Two beings existed within this: Apsu, who represents the fresh waters, and Tiamat, described as a mighty dragon, who represents the salt waters. The two conjoin and from them spring a host of deities, including another Ea, here a god of wisdom and magic. Apsu finds the new generation unruly and noisy and seeks to destroy them, but Ea is too quick and destroys Apsu instead. Tiamat is horrified by this and enlists the help of Ea's half-brother Kingu, engendering a tribe of monsters. Meanwhile, Apsu is lost in the sweet waters beneath the earth where he sires Marduk, who swiftly grows to manhood and leads an assault on Ea, Kingu and the rebel gods. All are destroyed, along with Tiamat, whose body is dismembered and used to create earth and heaven. Marduk now rules supreme.

From here the tale travelled on until it appeared in perhaps its best-known form in the Greek myths of Okeanos, Kronos and Zeus. Here, following references in Homer and later Hesiod's *Theogony*, we learn that the sea is again the origin of all things, but that it is the earth, Gaia, who first gives birth to Ouranos ('Heaven'), marries him and begets a race of giants known as the Titans, including Okeanos ('Ocean') and Kronos ('Time'). When Ouranos acts harshly to his children, Gaia conspires with her last-born, Kronos, to emasculate his father with a jagged sickle. The god's severed genitals fall into the sea and from them is born the love goddess Aphrodite.

Kronos, now enthroned as the ruler of heaven and married to the Titaness Rhea, lives in fear that his offspring will turn upon him as he did upon his own father. He, therefore, consumes his children at birth until the youngest, Zeus, is saved by his mother, who replaces him with a stone. Kronos eats this without noticing, and Zeus is free to grow to full godhood by being dangled by the nymph Amalthea on a golden thread between the earth and the heavens, which prevents Kronos from seeing him. (This sounds very much like a variant of the celestial pole story.) Zeus then enlists allies from among the fallen gods and Titans, and together they attack and overcome Kronos, who is forced to regurgitate his children. Together, Zeus and his allies assume control of heaven, and Kronos is banished (some say to the Blessed Isles, which, according to later traditions, are identified with Britain). The Titans are sent to Tartarus, where they are kept imprisoned.

In the Iranian variant of the 'Kingship in Heaven', Yima (Jamshid), the story of the Sword in the Ground is combined with that of the 'Kingship in Heaven', showing that the ancients knew the tales went together. This means that the stories were probably transmitted in the same way: through diffusion. As the story begins Yima is already the First King of Heaven. His solution to saving humanity was to put a golden seal on the ground and press a long dagger through it into the ground. After he created the Underworld, he was deposed and sawn in two. The next Iranian generation featured Zohak, the monstrous son of Wadag, who conceived him through an incestuous relationship. He was chained to a mountain for wanting to murder his grandson. Then Fereydun came along and killed Zohak, and the new world order was established.

A few centuries later the Phoenicians developed a version of the myth where Eliun was the god who repairs Chaos.

The next god, Epigeius (Sky), was driven out of heaven and emasculated. Then along came El, who emasculated himself, probably because his wife was the goddess Astarte and that was something priests of her religion did. El was eventually deposed by the weather god, Ba'al, who was represented by a Golden Bull and the sun because he rose from the Underworld each day and returned there every night. A variant of this story shows up in the Old Testament of the Bible when the Hebrew people turn to the worship of a Golden Calf while Moses is off receiving the Ten Commandments.

Table 2. Iranian Tales

In the Beginning	First King	Second King	Weather God
Ahura Mazda Vivanghvant	Yima (Jamshid) Yimaha (sister and wife)	Zohak (Monstrous son born of Wadag, his, mother, from incest)	Ferydun
	Puts golden seal on ground and presses it into the earth with a long dagger; sawn in two; takes men and animals into enclosure to protect them from harsh winters sent to cure evil/overpopulation		
	Rules the Underworld (Glory seized by Mithra in another story)	Chained to Mountain	Slays Zohak (or chains him to a mountain)

We do not have the Canaanite version of the 'Kingship in Heaven' in its original form, but we can reconstruct it from the other variants as well as from the Phoenicians, who were related to the Canaanites.[16] The variant carried by the Israelites is the one we know the most about because the stories were incorporated into the sacred texts of the Jews and the Christians. Originally preserved through oral transmission among the Israelites, they were first written down during the Babylonian captivity of the sixth century BCE. While the Jews are known for their monotheistic religion, things didn't start out that way.

Table 3. Phoenician Tales

In the Beginning	First King	Second King	Weather God
Eliun	Epigeius (Sky) Earth	El (Elus; Heads assembly of gods) Astarte (Ashera; wears bull head)	Ba'al (associated with bulls and Underworld)
	Gods, including El	Monstrous children: Titanides (daughters) and sons)	
	Overthrown by El		

Around the third century BCE a text called the *Septuagint* was composed in Greek, probably in Egypt and perhaps even at the library of Alexandria. This was an attempt to take all of the variants of the *Torah*, the *Pentateuch* and other texts that were floating around, and combine them into an edited form with the only god being called 'Yahweh'. The editors, however, missed a few places in the text where they left the names of some of the deities from an earlier pantheon and bits of their tales. In the story as we have it, El, whose name unhelpfully means 'God', and his unnamed wife create the waters and earth out of chaos. They have children, among them Samael, the angel of death according to the *Talmud*, who is associated with either the bull Taurus or the ram Aries. El leads a Council of Gods, who, like the Hurrian Anu, did not much like his children and promised to destroy them.

Two stories seem to have covered this part, with one telling how El sent a flood but let Noah save some of humanity and the other relating how El's son Samael rebelled against him, hoping to make himself the King of Heaven. Another god, also named El, defeats Samael and throws him into Hell where, according to the Kabbalah, he sires demons with his partner, Lilith. The second El is the storm god, and his partner is the fertility goddess Ashera.[17] He rules the assembly of gods until Yahweh replaces him in the texts.

And then there is Egypt. Most of what we know about Egypt's ever-changing pantheon comes from images inscribed in a variety of temples and pyramids. Many of the deities, as with the Babylonians, are local, centred on specific cities. Here the myth mostly consists of an assembly of gods and goddesses sharing each other's stories, and the Egyptians seemed to have liked it that way. Hathor, for instance, is a goddess associated with cows whose inscriptions from the time of Hatshepsut state quite clearly she was imported through Punt, yet she appears in the role of Isis when not taking on the role of Ra's wife.

Table 4. Canaanite Reconstruction

In the Beginning	First King	Second King	Weather God
Chaos	El (Sky) Astarte/Ashera	Samael (Bull; also associated with Aries, the Goat, who also stands for the Golden Fleece)	El Asherah
	Angels (terrifying children), including Samael	Rebels against father. Sires demons with Lilith	Defeats the Golden Bull (Samael)
		Hyper-sexual; thrown into the Underworld	Replaced by Yahweh in the conversion to monotheism.

The oldest stories indicate that Ra rose out of the waters of Chaos and proceeded to spend millennia trying to impose order on the mess that was the world. He either replaces an even older god, Atum, or rules with him or combines with him into Atum-Ra.[18] Somewhere in there one of them, usually Atum, sires the Ennead, a group of nine deities worshipped at Heliopolis. They consisted of the sun god Atum, his children Shu and Tefnut and Tefnut, their children Geb and Nut, and their children Osiris, Set, Isis and Nephys. An older version of Horus makes up the ninth. These rowdy gods continually rebel against Ra until he decides to go sit in the sky as the sun god and be done with them.

Out of this primordial stew of myths in Egypt the clearest, best-known and most detailed narrative sequence surfaces during the Old Kingdom, *c.* 2686–2181 BCE. In this Osiris and his sister-wife, Isis, take over as the rulers of the gods. Osiris' brother, Set, opposes him and tears Osiris to pieces, throwing him into either the sea or the Nile, where his genitals are eaten by either a crab or a catfish. Isis manages to find all of the pieces, except for the really important one, and to put her husband back together again. She uses her magic to give him a golden phallus, and he sires a son, Horus, on her. She escapes to an island with Horus (echoing the way Zeus was raised on an island), while Osiris essentially becomes the Lord of the Underworld, along with or taking over from Anubis, who is Set's son but dates back to the much older pantheon that included Atum.

Horus grows up and takes revenge on Set. The two engage in numerous competitions, and in one Horus' semen winds up inside Set after Horus successfully prevented Set from ejaculating into him. Eventually they call a truce and Set becomes king over the desert while Horus gets all the Nile valley and delta. In other words, Set, who is described as a storm god, ends up on the side of the Nile reserved for the burial of the dead.

Table 5. Egyptian Tales

In the Beginning	First King	Second King	Weather God
Chaos (Water) Ra (Sun/Land) Hathor (imported cow goddess; shares stories with Isis)	Osiris Isis (severed head replaced by head of cow)	Set (Storm god)	Horus (sky god; eyes are the sun and moon)
Shu, Geb	Child: Horus	Monstrous children: Anubis	

(Cont'd)

In the Beginning	First King	Second King	Weather God
Gods rebel against Ra; he retreats to sky and passes nightly through the Duat, an Otherworld.	Body torn apart by Set, reassembled by Isis except for genitals, replaced with golden phallus; penis was eaten by a crab (Cancer?) or a catfish. Rules the Underworld as does Set's son.	Hyper-sexual god of the Underworld. Horus rebels against him; contests ensue, including one of trying to get semen inside each other. Winds up as exiled king in desert land where the dead are buried.	Becomes king of the fertile lands of the Nile.

These are but some of the complex of creation myths collected under the broad heading of the 'Kingship in Heaven'. Each in its own way reflects the movement of the heavens being replaced by the actions of the gods and their endless efforts for supremacy.

The pattern of distribution for the legend of the Sword in the Stone and its variants suggests that these tales were also transmitted by diffusion from one culture to another rather than by parallel development or by independent invention among the cultures where the tale appears. The starting point seems to be within Eurasia, with the tale carried out from that nexus across the Caucasus Mountains to the Hittites, and thence to lands across Eurasia and even as far south as Yorubaland.

The diaspora of the Indo-European-speaking peoples occurred in three movements.[19] The first took place around 2025–2000 BCE and included the proto-Tocharians, whose

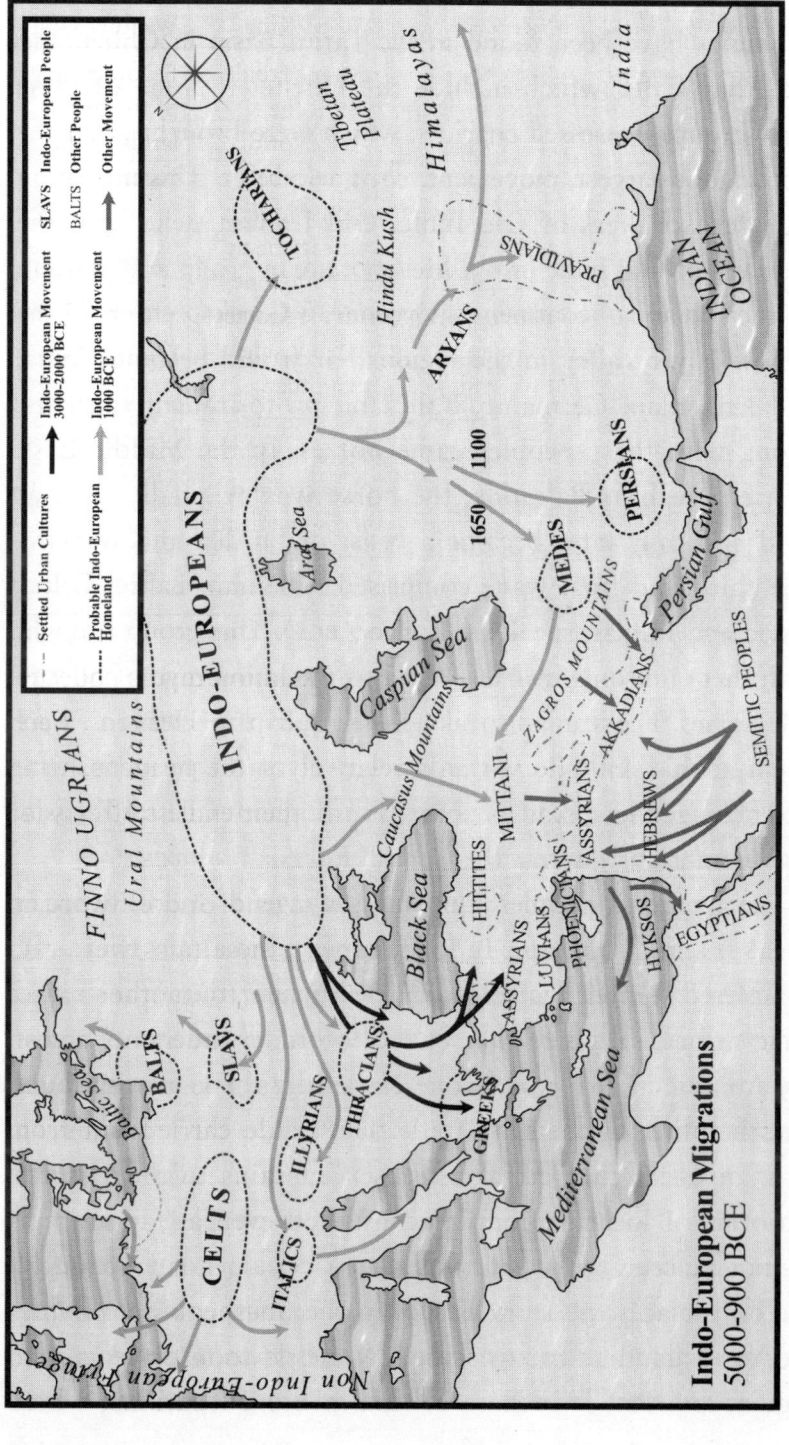

Map 1. Migrations of the Indo-European World. (W. Kinghan)

mummies have been found in the Tarim Basin in China, and the Anatolians, which include the Hittites.[20] None of these early groups possessed chariots, which were brought in by the second, and largest, movement, *circa* 1600 BCE. This migration included speakers of Old Indic, Old Iranian (who split the speakers of Old Indic into a Mesopotamian group and a group on the Indian subcontinent), Mycenaean Greeks, settlers in the Yellow River valley in the region that would become China, and Armenian, Germanic, Italic and proto-Iranian speakers. Along with these peoples came horses. In the Middle East, in areas such as Palestine, the horse was originally used as food and only later became a beast of burden and warfare. The third and final wave comprised Albanian, Baltic, Celtic, Slavic and Iranian speakers (*c.* 1500 BCE). This group brought with them not only chariots but also the knowledge of how to ride horses. The Iranian speakers, especially the Scythians, were adept at this skill and within a relatively short period of time had managed to spread as nomads throughout Central Eurasia, most importantly across the Central Eurasian steppes.[21]

The impacted peoples – previous waves of Indo-European speakers and the non-Indo-European speakers they had conquered – after centuries of development then transmitted their stories, including that of the Sword in the Stone, across the Atlantic in two waves: one carried by the Conquistadores and the other by the slave trade. The key to this transmission was an event that could be observed in the sky from the majority of locations occupied by these peoples, but which cannot be seen at locations outside a certain range. Tellingly, the only places the story occurs in the Southern Hemisphere are Yorubaland and areas settled by the slaves taken from that region, and that is because of transmission, which leapt over several latitude parallels to get there. Normally the tale loses all meaning outside the zone of the Central Eurasian Culture Complex and its peripheral states, though the descendants of the people who first told it kept passing it along, even after the story had lost all meaning for them, probably by way of a trade route called the Iron Road, which existed before the more famous Silk Road.[22] This is how we find everyone focusing on Arthur pulling the sword out of an anvil atop a stone rather than being concerned with what the image of the Sword in the Stone actually meant.

Let us begin our journey, then, by looking first at the main forms of the story as it appears and spreads across Eurasia, in a narrow band from one side of the continent to the other, from there to the outliers of Yorubaland and Japan, and then across the Atlantic to the Americas. From here we can begin to unravel the true meaning of the Sword in the Stone.

PART I
THE SWORD
IN THE STONE

I

THE HITTITE SWORD GOD

We have to travel a long way back in time to find the origin of the Sword in the Stone. The trail begins in Anatolia (modern-day Turkey), where the Hittites arrived, *c.* 2230 BCE, from the south Russian steppes, the homeland of the Indo-European-speaking peoples.[1] Many Indo-European peoples worshipped a sword god, but the oldest evidence of those associated with the Sword in the Stone comes from the Hittites.[2] By 1600 BCE these people had established a socially superior stratum over the Hattians, who spoke neither Indo-European nor Semitic languages and who had conquered the Semitic-speaking Hurrians sometime around 2300 BCE, about three-quarters of a century before the Hittites invaded. Though in control for only a short time as empires go, the Hurrians had a great impact on their conquerors, so much so that some of the traditions are referred to as Hurro-Hittite or Hittite-Hurrian. In fact, some of their words and lore survived in the Hittite traditions.

The major evidence for the existence of the Hittite sword god is found in a sacred complex at Yazılıkaya near the original Hittite capitol of Hattusha. The sanctuary was originally a Hattian site for the worship of Underworld deities but was then redesigned by the Hittites.[3] The sculptures and Hurrian glosses were added during the reign of one of the last Hittite kings, Tudhaliya IV (r. 1237–1209 BCE), whose mortuary chapel forms part of the complex.[4] Notably, the chapel is unfinished, which means that the sword god was a late addition to the pantheon and, therefore, Hittite.

Although there are several structures in front of the *adyton*, the holiest part of the Yazılıkaya temple, the heart of the site consists of two crevices in the natural rock formation that are open to the sky. Though we refer to these openings as 'chambers' because that is the terminology the literature uses, the word 'chamber' gives the false impression that these areas are caves. In reality they are smaller than this, and, rather than being places for large gatherings, the ability to view the sky from within them is absolutely critical to the understanding of this monument and is a feature often ignored in discussions of the site.

Although some scholars argue that the mathematical precision of the Babylonian Zodiac may not have yet been established, Chamber A gives lie to that notion.[5] At the very least the Hittites, and possibly the Hurrians before them, had started to pick out celestial patterns before the Babylonians came on the scene. While much has been made of the Babylonian astrologers dividing the Zodiac into twelve portions in the fifth century BCE, we suggest that the division occurred much earlier. At the very least the Hittites associated the number twelve with the stars by the reign of Tudhaliya IV.

Chamber A is considerably larger than Chamber B. Upon entering Chamber A, the observer stares directly across an open space at the images of seven deities who are all associated

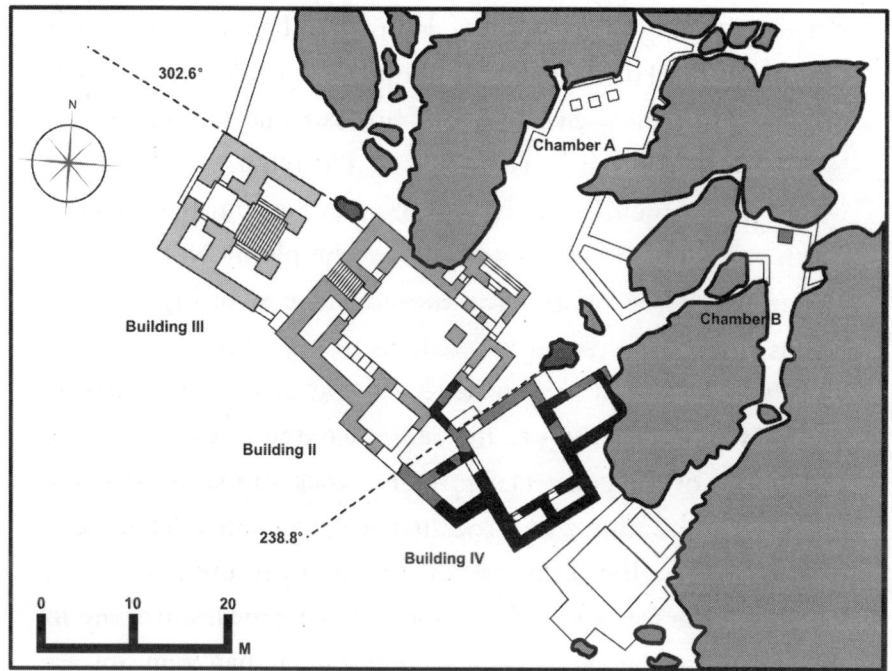

Fig. 1. Plan showing the location of Chambers A and B as well as the three phases of temple construction. The gatehouse (Building 111) is directed at the sunset during summer solstice. The north-western wall of Building IV is aligned with the sunset during the winter solstice.

with the heavens.[6] These are Teshub, the two bulls Seri and Hurri (Day and Night, from the Hurrian pantheon; or perhaps Taurus depicted conquering the Gemini, the Divine Twins, of which more in chapter 9), Teshub's wife Hebat, their son Sarruma, their daughter Alanzu (Hattic pantheon) and their granddaughter Tarhunt (Hattic pantheon).

On the right-hand wall, nineteen goddesses and one god (Sarruma) march to meet Hebat. On the left wall, twenty-eight gods, one goddess and twelve unarmed divine runners proceed toward Teshub. The processions are mostly in the order of the original Hurrian pantheon even though they were created by Hittite artists – except, that is, for the twelve divine runners.

This grouping of deities is a complete mishmash of origins, caused by the Hittite habit of adopting divinities from other peoples into their own pantheon, much as the Romans would later absorb the religious figures of virtually everyone with whom they came in contact. Teshub, the 'Zeus' of the Hurrian pantheon, is only loosely analogous to the Hittite weather god, Tarhu, yet it is probably Tarhu whom the main deity in the reconstructed procession is intended to represent.[7] Yazılıkaya was once the site of a fresh-water spring,[8] which designated it as a holy spot. Offerings to the deities were thrown into holes,[9] and stories of the gods refer to them as also disappearing into holes.[10] Thus, Tarhu was associated with underground sources of water rather than with water from the sky.[11] As such, he was the god of the Underworld. He was, indeed, the closest thing in the Hittite pantheon to another deity who would soon appear on the scene as a sword god, and he became a gloss for that figure.

Among the Hittites, a local deity was often represented by 'a weapon, an animal or a *huwasi*-stone, an upright stela set on a carved base', so it was natural for them to adopt a sword god and represent him this way.[12] In a temple, 'occasionally a deity ... would be represented by his sacred animal ... or by a weapon such as a sword or spear'.[13]

Chamber A is thought to have been used for the Hittite New Year celebration, which occurred in spring, most likely at or near the equinox, 21 March.[14] During this festival, the Hittite gods were said to gather at the house of the weather god, and it is this event that most scholars think is represented by the processions in Chamber A. In all, the display seems to represent a giant calendar based on the sun that the Hittite priests used to track the solar year and lunar months.[15]

Chamber B is accessed through a crevice that was widened to allow access to the space beyond. Like Chamber A, Chamber B is open to the sky. Unlike Chamber A, Chamber B was a private space: Tudhaliya IV's mortuary chapel. The chapel contains a depiction of the king with his patron deity, the Hurrian Sarruma. There is evidence that birds were sacrificed at the site, and there is also evidence of burials, which makes this chapel a 'graveyard' while the house of the weather god in Chamber A represents the Underworld.[16] So something slightly different is going on in this space than in Chamber A. It is still associated with death, but something closer to the mortal world than to the Underworld. The same is true in other traditions where the Sword in the Stone is frequently associated with a graveyard.

The smaller chamber may have been the site of a spring ritual that differed from the New Year celebration. There is a Hittite festival that was held at roughly this time of the year. The Hittite sword god, Zababa, was worshipped under the signs of Aries and Taurus, which ruled the sky of the Northern Hemisphere from 21 March through 21 May, and a war god is an excellent description of the sword god. During this festival, a ram and a bull were sacrificed to the sword god beneath a tree (the *eya*). We know of the *eya*-tree from the 'Edict of Tudhaliya IV', the king featured in Chamber B, with the sword god, at Yazılıkaya.

The *eya*-tree was the Hittite version of the World Tree, which represents the celestial pole (as mentioned in the Introduction) in the context of all these deities. The *eya*-tree was used to fashion spears by the Hittites, so it is odd to find a deity associated with a sword rather than a tree or spear in this image. A clue, however, may lie in the detail that, although the *eya*-tree was usually placed on the altars of various deities as part of their worship, the sacrifice of the bull and ram to the sword god took place on an altar *above* the *eya*-tree, which may represent the shifting of the celestial pole (the World Tree) from Taurus into Aries.

As we shall see, this is the same configuration that Herodotus reported among the Scythians in their worship of 'Ares', their sword god: specifically, an altar above a pile of wood. Yet for the Hittites, the sword was embedded in stone.

What we see at Yazılıkaya is typical of what happens when an outsider god comes into an area and takes over. The outside deity synchronises to the closest deity in the existing pantheon. The champion of this practice was probably the Christian church, whose saints took over any number of local deities. The early church learned this custom from the Romans, and long before that the Hittites were playing at the same game.

On the same wall as the image of Sarruma and Tudhaliya IV in Chamber B is a sword god. His head forms the pommel of a sword. Two lions form the hilt. The rest of his body is a sword, which is shown as embedded in the stone wall. So, here is a king in a graveyard in conjunction with a god represented as a sword who is shown as embedded in stone, which has significant similarities to Arthur pulling a sword out of a stone in a graveyard. This chamber appears to be dedicated to the stars, and as such, the sword god is likely a figure from the sky.[17] The sword god, however, is not included in the official Hittite state pantheon, which is depicted in Chamber A. He appears to be one of the last additions to the site since the figure to his left is unfinished.

Across from the sword god, in Chamber B, the twelve running deities from Chamber A are repeated, but this time they all carry sickle-shaped swords, whereas they are unarmed in the first chamber. This is from a story where the deities use swords to sever themselves from the sky.[18] It is reminiscent of Zeus being suspended between Heaven and Earth by a golden thread in the 'Kingship in Heaven' story from the Greeks, and it may hint at a connection between the runners and Aries, the sheep whose fleece was of gold, which was aligned opposite the sword god on the celestial pole after Thuban moved from the position of the pole star, something we will discuss in chapter 9. Keep in mind that the Zodiac has Twelve Signs, Christ had Twelve Disciples and Charlemagne and King Arthur both had Twelve Companions.[19] The twelve runners with the swords are on the western wall, and 'west' is the traditional direction of the Otherworld, the Land of the Dead, in many Indo-European traditions. So once again, we have the connection with a graveyard.

The Twelve Companions

As J. G. Macqueen pointed out, 'the principle weapon employed [from Hittite chariots] was the stabbing spear',[20] but the Hittite soldiers of the Anatolian hills wielded a slashing-sword, which was replaced by 'a long cutting-weapon with a straight blade by the end of the second millennium'.[21] Unlike the Kalybes – the Scythian smiths from the juncture of the Black Sea and the Caucasus Mountains whom the Romans considered to be the first people to forge iron – the early Hittites could not make good iron on a regular schedule.[22] This knowledge would only come later, and with it came the development of the Iron Road. As we saw, this route was a precursor to the Silk Road, which spanned Central Eurasia.

The swords carried by the twelve runners in Chamber B resemble the short, crescent-shaped swords decorated with animal heads that Hittite warriors carried in ceremonies rather than in battle.[23] Although the gods carry the swords in this image, in the Hittite texts they are described as embedded. The Hittite axe carried by Sarruma has 'ribbing round the shaft-hole [that] is a feature' from, among other places, the northern Caucasus area, while the axe's blade 'is of a type which can be paralleled only in the Caucasus region'.[24] The imagery is saying that the story and the knowledge of forging iron that went with it came from the Caucasus Mountains.

As we mentioned above, the weather god in Hittite tradition was associated with holes in rocks and underground sources of water.[25] He was, as Hilary Deighton proved, worshipped underground.[26] This is not what is happening at Yazılıkaya, however, where Chamber B, like Chamber A, is open to the sky and where the emphasis is on celestial deities. So, in this context the 'weather god' is probably a gloss for a sword god who was connected with a graveyard and who was worshipped by the sacrifice of bulls and sheep.[27]

In 2160 BCE the celestial pole shifted from Taurus into Aries, the bull and the ram, the two signs that were presided over by the Hittite sword god. The Scythian sword god, however, was only associated with the sign of Aries, demonstrating that the pole had moved solidly into that sign by the time their kingdom held sway, in the ninth or eighth century BCE. As we shall see in greater detail later on, this god (who has no recorded name) was the divine warrior who reached across the circle of the Zodiac and embedded his weapon in the opposite sign.[28] For the Hittites, this sign included a stone altar, known to the Greeks and Romans as the *Ara*, which is associated with Libra.

Elizabeth Wayland Barber and Paul Barber have referred to the image of the sword god at Yazılıkaya as 'the divine spirit of this Sword in the Stone', and in doing so, they are on the right track.[29] The steppe sword god, whom Herodotus called Ares, was not himself the celestial ram, but was represented by its story, just as the Greek Jason can be represented by the Golden Fleece. The twelve figures associated with the sword god, then, may have nothing at all to do with Underworld deities of Chamber A. Instead, they may represent the twelve months of the year, or even the twelve signs of the Zodiac, and the 'the twelve gods of the crossroads'[30] might not be underground at all but rather in the sky.

There are a couple of supportive texts that may give us a clue as to how the Hittites thought of this particular sword god. One states that the weather god chased at least three deities into the Underworld and limited them to the sacrifices of birds, reserving for himself the sacrifice of the bull and ram ('ox and sheep').[31] Another text, *The Prayer of Kantuzzili*, tells how Underworld gods were shaped from clay into the form of swords and implanted in the ground.[32] In a still later text, the swords are bronze and are associated with the Babylonian Underworld deity of Nergal, who was contemporary with the Hittite sword god and connected with the planet Mars and lions.[33] A bronze sword similar to that at Yazılıkaya was found in the city of Diyarbakir, today in south-eastern Turkey. This sword was an offering to Nergal at his temple.[34] Here, then, we have a situation where Nergal probably absorbed a story about embedded bronze swords and a sword god who was associated with the Underworld, rams, bulls and lions. These swords are mentioned in conjunction with the twelve gods of the crossroads, so there was a sense that the sword god and the Twelve Companions belonged together.[35]

Forging Iron

When swords began to be made of iron instead of bronze and when the story of the Sword in the Stone was transmitted to Samaria in Mesopotamia, a stone throne or altar was added to the tale. This may be *Ara*, the altar that is associated with the constellation of Libra. The knowledge of how to forge iron into swords travelled with the story of a sword god whose priest(s), accompanied by twelve companions, either pulled a sword from or plunged it into an altar as a sign of the god's presence. It was this deity that the Hittites probably brought with them from the Caucasus Mountains. He was distinctly different from the rest of the deities in the Hurro-Hittite pantheon. On the steppes, where he was described by Herodotus as Ares, he stayed fixed in one place with an immovable temple while the rest of the gods were mobile. At Yazılıkaya in Anatolia he got his own chamber and was literally embedded in stone.

Although the Hittites have traditionally been known for their use of iron, they were not the people who invented the practice of forging it into swords. That honour goes to the Kalybes, the renowned smiths of the Caucasus region, where both the Hurrians and Hittites had their origins. Laroche suggested that the Hittite words for iron – *kiklu* and *hapalki* (steel) – were connected to the Kalybes of the Pontus.[36] The Kalybian smiths used 'local deposits of iron ore' to produce weapons 'on a scale that had never been possible with bronze'.[37] The Kalybes also had access to black sands, rich in magnetite, which could be smelted.[38] Although there is a lot of folklore about the forging of swords from meteorites, as well as the presence of nickel 'taken to indicate the meteoric origin of iron',[39] the iron smelted from these other sources could be nickel-bearing as well. The Hittites, therefore, most likely got their knowledge of forging iron from the Caucasian Kalybes.[40]

Despite folklore to the contrary, there is no evidence that 'the Hittites owed their dominant position to their monopoly of the production of the secret weapon called iron'.[41] They seem to have picked up something else, however: the idea that the sword god could be represented by an iron sword. The steppe variant of this sword god presides over the forging of iron, though he is unnamed; nor could we find any images of him. His tale was probably part of the process of the transmission of the knowledge of how to forge iron. This happened toward the end of the Hittite Kingdom, which explains why the image is a late addition to the chapel and absent from the official pantheon. The sword god may have assimilated the Hittite weather god because of their shared connection with the Underworld and similar rituals.

The Hittite version of the Sword in the Stone story, then, has several elements in common with the Arthurian variant. Both feature an embedded sword in a graveyard. Both swords are associated with a king. The twelve runners in the Hittite variant parallel the Twelve Knights of the Round Table in Arthurian tradition. Also, the anvil of the Arthurian variant preserves the connection with the forging of iron. The tales are clearly part of the same tradition, yet, by placing the image of the sword god in conjunction with celestial deities at Yazılıkaya, the Hittites preserved an association that the Arthurian variant has lost. They still knew that the tale of the Sword in the Stone had something to do with the stars.

2

THE GREEK SWORD BENEATH
THE STONE

The next chapter in the story of the Sword in the Stone takes us forward into the classical period and specifically to ancient Greece. Here we will focus on the Indo-European sword hero tradition and look at what Scott Littleton considered to be the principal Greek reflex, the great Athenian hero Theseus (Θησεύς).

At about this period, when the Hittites invaded Anatolia, a second wave of emigrees from north of the Black Sea rode in to overlay the peoples already settled in ancient Greece. With them they brought gods that were not part of the original pantheon, most notably Poseidon – the god of earthquakes, volcanoes, and horses before he took over the religion of Okeanos (Ὠκεανός), the god of the ocean. They also brought the story of the Sword in the Stone, but they had split it in two and changed some of the details. Additionally, with them came a new form of sword, designed for slashing and with a flanged tang.

The Greek variant of the Sword in the Stone narrative appears principally in the tales of the hero Theseus.[1] Known as an abductor of women and a fighter against half-men/half-beasts,[2] he kidnaped Helen of Troy, Ariadne of Naxos and Persephone, the daughter of Zeus. His cult was established in shrines by the eighth century BCE, and he became a Pan-Hellenic hero by the mid-seventh century BCE.[3]

Theseus first appears as the son of either Poseidon or Aegeus in Bacchylides' *Ode 17*, which dates to the mid-fifth century BCE.[4] Like Odin from Germanic myth, Theseus was an 'unnatural, illegitimate foreigner' who carried a spear (Bacchylides *Ode 18* l.49) and wore a cloak (Bacchylides *Ode 18* l.54).[5]

An important part of the Theseus story is the motif of the Bear's Son, in which a hero with a magical sword descends to the Underworld. This appears in the Germanic 'Beowulf', which we will discuss in chapter 7, while in Greek tradition it split off into the story of Kallisto.[6] Kallisto was one of Artemis' nymphs, who had the misfortune to catch Zeus' eye. Zeus rapes her, and, when Artemis discovers that Kallisto is pregnant, she turns the unlucky nymph into a bear. Kallisto gives birth to a son, who is called (among other things) Arkas, thus enabling the Arkadians to take their name from him. Arkas is raised to be a great hunter, who eventually corners his mother in bear form. Zeus sets Kallisto in the stars as a bear, Ursa Major, and turns Arkas into either the star Arcturus (also rendered Arkturus) or the entire constellation, which we now know as Boötes but which the Greeks sometimes called Arcturus after its brightest star.[7] The star has been known by this name for at least 3,000 years,[8] and the story reappears as a parallel connection with Arthur, as we shall see in the next chapter.

What the Greek texts preserved in the case of the Kallisto narrative that other versions did not is evidence that they knew they were talking about a story written in the stars. In the case of the Greek tale, the sword hero's story appears in two major stories (three if you count Kallisto): that of Jason and the Golden Fleece and that of Theseus and the Minotaur.[9] Jason gets the fleece of the ram, which we saw referenced in Hittite rituals, and Theseus gets the bull in the form of the Minotaur. No mention is made of Jason's sword, but Theseus inherits a sword from his father. Both heroes have a pair of sandals that prove their birthright, and both are, for better or worse, involved with the god Poseidon.

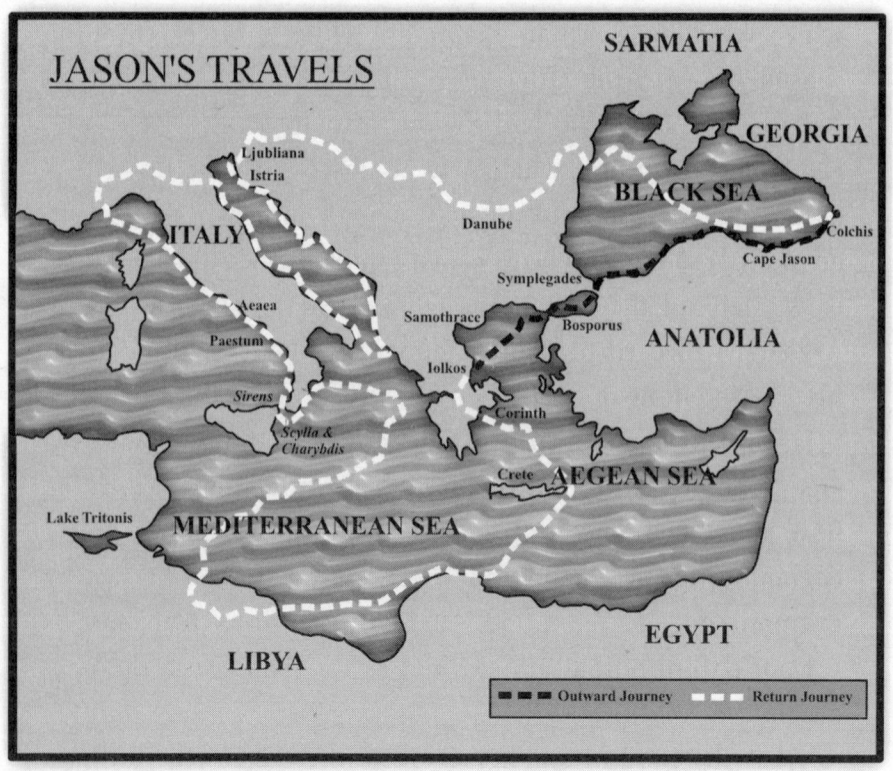

Map 2. Jason's travels. (W. Kinghan)

Jason's tale is recorded in the late third century BCE by Apollonius of Rhodes in his *Argonautica*. Jason's father is killed in Thessaly by his half-brother King Pelias of Iolcus, but Jason is saved by his mother, who has him raised in secrecy by the centaur Chiron, whose foster father is Apollo. (These sun gods will keep cropping up.) Pelias is told by an oracle to 'beware a man wearing only one sandal'.[10] On cue, Jason shows up at the games Pelias is holding in honour of Poseidon, wearing only one sandal, having lost the other when helping Hera, who was disguised as an old woman, to cross a river. Pelias sends the young hero on the Quest for the Golden Fleece, believing that he will be killed along the way. The Golden Fleece itself comes from a flying golden ram, suggesting a stellar connection in the story, namely the constellation of Aries.

Jason sets sail with the Divine Twins (Castor and Pollux), Herakles, and other semi-divine characters, several of whom have constellations named after them. Jason's first stop is on the coast of Anatolia, where he encounters a collection of women ruled by a queen. Herakles finally convinces the Argonauts to carry on with their quest, but not before Jason sires twins on the queen.

Jason next lands on the shores of Propontus, an inland sea along the coast of Anatolia that separates the Aegean Sea from the Black Sea. After some misadventures and a tragic beginning, the Argonauts sail on their way for their second attempt.

Jason's third port is at Salmydessus, in Thrace, on the shore of the Black Sea. Here Zeus gets involved, sending harpies to spoil any food or water presented to King Phineus, who is either the son or grandson of Agenor[11] and to whom Apollo gave the gift of prophecy. It is worth noting that Phineus' second wife was Scythian, the daughter of King Dardanus, who is sometimes scrambled with the ancestor of the Trojans by the same name. Like the unfortunate Prometheus who gave man fire, Phineus tells men about the future, hence the harpies. Jason solves the problem by killing the harpies, and Phineus tells the Argonauts how to get to their next port.

The Argonauts sail straight through the Symplegades, a pair of rocks, one on the European side of the Bosporus and the other on the Asian side. The cliffs repeatedly clash together, until the Greek heroes, following Phineus' advice, manage to run the gauntlet and pass through safely. After this, the rocks stop clashing, though they remain a navigational hazard.

From there, the Argonauts sail to a port on the northern part of the Black Sea that is now occupied by Georgia, adjacent to what was then Sarmatia. Here we are back in an area of north-eastern Iranian-speaking peoples.

Medea, a granddaughter of the sun god Helios and therefore semi-divine, now takes over as Jason's guide, instructing him in ways to defeat the challenges set for him. She reveals how to yoke a pair of fire-breathing oxen, which can be compared to the first of three golden objects that descended from the sky to the ancient Scythians (the yoke and plow) and which serve as one of Jason's versions of the bull motifs that we noted earlier among the Hittites. He uses the oxen to plow a field into which he sows dragons' teeth, which sprout into a group of warriors.[12] These are bodies from the earth, bringing in the graveyard motif again. Jason hurls a stone into their midst, and they kill each other. Medea now provides Jason with a potion to put to sleep the dragon that is guarding the Golden Fleece. He steals the fleece and escapes with Medea.

They pass the sirens, who cause Odysseus so much trouble, by the simple expediency of having Orpheus, one of those legendary members of the crew who traced his roots to Thrace, play his harp louder than the creatures could sing. Medea gets them past the bronze man Telos at Crete (who was throwing large stones at them) by putting him to sleep with a spell and removing the one bolt that holds him together, causing him to bleed to death. We will encounter the motif of the metal man among other peoples who tell the story of the Sword in the Stone.

Eventually the *Argo* sails into port in Greece, and the heroes go their separate ways. This is followed by a lot of bloodshed and treason, which ends with the sun god Helios lending Medea his golden chariot, which was pulled by dragons, in order to escape. Jason remains with Achilles' father, Peleus, for a while, then meets a lonely death, crushed by the *Argo's* decaying stern.

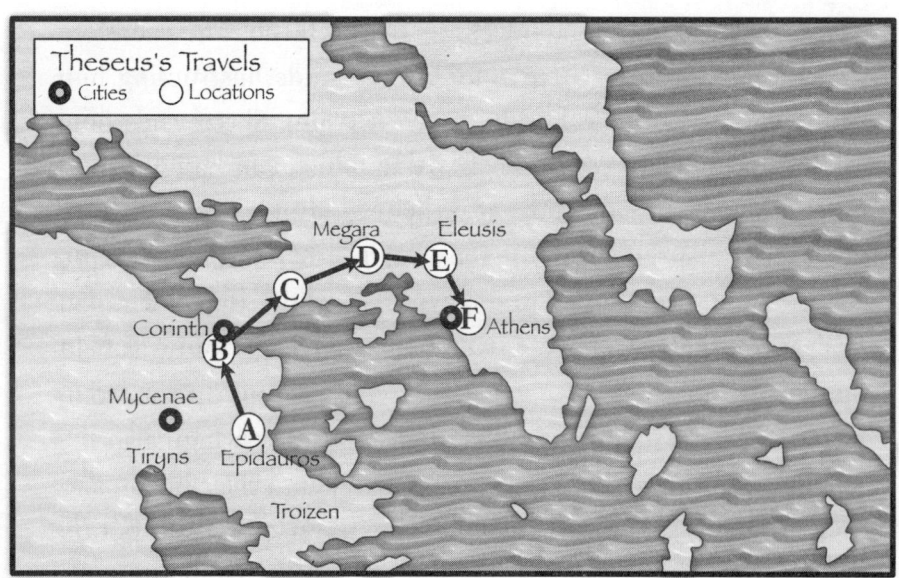

Map 3. Theseus' travels. (W. Kinghan)

So here we have a hero, minus the sword and stone but in possession of a pair of sandals and a fleece from the flying Golden Ram, who is represented by the constellation Aries. There is a good deal of steppe nomad material, and the tale can be traced deep into antiquity at a period roughly contemporary with the Hittite sword god. The voyage of the Argonauts actually reverses the route the ancestors of the Greeks would have taken, albeit on land, journeying from the north side of the Black Sea into what became the Greek mainland, and carrying the story with them. The original pattern of travel is also told of a Nart from the Caucasus Mountains, who serves as the Jason figure in stories of the descendants of the Alano-Sarmatians.

This brings us to the story of Theseus.[13] His sword was not in a stone but rather under one. The primary sources for this legend are Plutarch (*Theseus*) and Apollodorus (*Bibliotheca*),[14] but the Greek variant of the Sword in the Stone occurs in the first of Plutarch's *Parallel Lives*, where the text pairs the tale of Theseus with that of Romulus, the mythical founder of Rome.

Plutarch was born around 50 CE, when Claudius was emperor of Rome.[15] His hometown was Chaeronea, which is located north-west of Thebes. He had a superb education, including extended study at Athens.[16] He served as 'deputy to the Roman governor of the province of Greece', traveling throughout Asia Minor and Egypt as well as Italy.[17] He died *c.* 120 CE. The *Lives* were composed after his retirement from public life, possibly during Trajan's reign (98–117 CE). Scholars have not been able to establish the original order of the pairs of lives,[18] so we do not know where the Theseus/Romulus set originally appeared in Plutarch's sequence. Although the author of the *Bibliotheca* has been identified from the ninth century CE onward as 'Apollodorus the Grammarian',[19] who lived *c.* 140 BCE, this identification has been shown to be incorrect.[20] The correct Apollodorus, 'Apollodorus the Athenian', probably wrote under the rulership of Hadrian (117–138 CE) or Severus Alexander (222–235 CE).[21] His account is thus considerably later than Plutarch's, but there is no significant reason to doubt that he was anything other than an Athenian, and he probably picked up the tale in Athens.[22] The manuscript tradition is actually from the fifteenth century and later, and we are forced to rely on Greeks in the Roman Empire for our accounts of the story.

As the tale begins, a friend of King Aegius of Athens arranges for him to sire a son on his daughter – with a little help from Poseidon. Having done his duty, Aegius takes off, leaving his sandals and sword beneath a stone and instructions for Aithra, Theseus' mother, to send the boy to him when he is able to lift the stone and free them.[23] When Theseus attains adulthood, his mother dutifully shows him the stone. Theseus moves the stone and claims his birthright, the sandals and the sword. In some variants, the sword and sandals are in a cache in the stone, so we do actually have an embedded sword in some instances. Note that here we see the first appearance of a woman who is a close relative at the moment when the hero carries out the feat, something Littleton called the motif of the 'Female Sword Bestower'.

Theseus' mother instructs him to take the sandals and sword to Aegius in Athens. Poseidon could have made the hero's journey across the Gulf of Argos easy, but Theseus, determined to prove himself, sets out overland. He chooses a long way around, north through the Argolid and across the Isthmus of Corinth into Attica – once more retracing the route the ancient Greeks would have taken to get to Athens. En route, he finds more than enough to keep him – and his newfound sword –

busy. The journey by land causes him to pass six entrances to the Underworld, which he uses, leaving a trail of bodies behind him, once more bringing the graveyard and the Land of the Dead into the tale.

Near Epidaurus, Theseus slays a brigand called Korynetes, or 'Club-Man'. Afterward, he appropriates – and later uses – the brigand's lethal club, a trait that was probably borrowed from the Herakles legend. Next, he kills Sinis, the 'Pine-Bender', so called because he regularly lashes his victims between two tied pine trees, which he then releases with predictable results. After that he hunts and kills the Grey Sow of Krommyon. When he reaches the vicinity of Megara, on the edge of Athens, Theseus slays another brigand, named Skeiron, who had a habit of throwing passersby off a cliff after compelling them to wash his feet. At Eleusis, he kills a formidable wrestler named Kerkyon and as he approaches Athens itself he manages to overcome Procrustes, who either lopped off his victims' limbs or stretched them to fit his infamous bed. Thus, by the time Theseus finally reaches Athens, he has already begun to establish himself as a sword hero.

After a narrow escape from being poisoned by Medea (Jason's former wife, just in case we were unclear that the two tales were connected), the young hero's sword and sandals reveal who he is, and his father happily recognises him as his son and heir. So here we have an embedded sword associated with a stone, a young hero, and graveyard entrances to the Underworld, with the boy acquiring his birthright by displaying his sandals, which is similar to Arthur achieving his birthright by pulling the sword from the Stone, which we will discuss more fully in the next chapter.

All goes well at first, but Theseus soon learns that Athens has a problem. The city had recently been resoundingly defeated by Minos, the king of Crete, and is obliged to send an annual tribute of seven young men and an equal number of maidens to be devoured by the monstrous Minotaur – half man, half bull – or to become lost and die of starvation in the famous Labyrinth of Knossos. With the help of Minos' daughter Ariadne, Theseus defeats the Minotaur and escapes the labyrinth using a golden thread provided by her, but despite her help and devotion to him, he abandons her on his way home. Note that, like Zeus' golden rope that connected him between the earth and sky, Theseus' thread connects him with the world of the Minotaur, littered with the dead sacrifices from Athens to the mortal world.

The rest of Theseus' career includes a series of much-needed institutional reforms in the government of his city – hence his name, which probably derives from the same root as Greek θεσμός ('institution') – and two significant heroic adventures. The first is the subduing of the ferocious Marathon Bull, which he brings back to Athens for sacrifice. Taken together with his killing of the Minotaur, this story suggests a parallel with another bull-sacrificing sword god: the most famous heroic bull slayer, the Roman god Mithras.

Mithras

Instead of telling the Jason and Theseus stories, the Romans told the tales of Mithras, who dates from the mid-first century BCE in Asia Minor. This ancient Iranian and later Greco-Roman god is a celestial deity who annually sacrificed a sacred bull, symbolic of spring,[24] but rather than associating him with the sun, a symbol that is clearly visible in his representations, we think he stood for the constellation Aries. Mithras' story, like Jason's, has astrological implications, since the bull represents the constellation Taurus and other animals that take part in the sacrifice also have astrological connotations. Theseus' capture and sacrifice of the Marathon Bull duplicates the iconography of Mithras in an image from a second- or third-century relief. There, to the left of the scene of Mithras slaying the bull, is a figure that most scholars have identified as Sol, the Roman sun.

We suggest that this figure developed from the chariot of Helios and that the image ties this story to that of the Golden Fleece. That Theseus and the Iranian deity – or at least his Greco-Roman persona – sprang from a common source is also a distinct possibility. Stories upon stories, but they all trace back to the same place and peoples: the Indo-European-speaking peoples north of the Black Sea.

While the best-known portrayals of the god Mithras show him plunging a knife or sword into a bull's neck, his early stories do not contain an embedded-sword motif. Plaques of a figure in Phrygian cap holding a knife over a bull have been found in the first century BCE in Crimea, but they may not be connected to Mithras' rites since they were discovered in a woman's tomb and women were not allowed in the all-male religion. The earliest pottery associated with the cult (80–120 CE) has been found in Germania Superior, Noricum and Judea, while dedications have been discovered in Germania Superior, Pannonia Superior, Rome and Moesia. Note that these locations are generally at the borders of the Roman Empire, signalling that this is a deity coming in from outside.

Mithras first appears without the Roman worship traits in the time of the Hittites in the mid-first century BCE in Asia Minor. The full-blown Roman mysteries are not attested until the mid-first century CE, and the *Mithraea*, the underground locations where Mithras was worshipped, do not begin appearing in the Roman Empire until the last quarter of the first century CE. Mithras' worship was favoured by soldiers, though many freedmen and slaves as well as senators participated.

Mithras' story has been reconstructed from art, literature and other sources. Images resembling the Hittite sword god show Mithras being born from a stone beside a river, wielding a sword in each hand. Others recall images of Theseus' slaying of the Marathon Bull. The underground places of worship were usually located near fresh water, often a stream. These details recall the Ossetian sword hero Soslan/Sosruko, who was born from a rock on a riverbank. One day Helios, the sun god, sent a raven to command Mithras to sacrifice a bull. Mithras obeyed, and several wonders happened, such as his cloak turning into the sky, including planets and stars. After other adventures, Mithras left the earth in Helios' chariot. The Romans were quite clear that they were telling a story about something that happened in the stars.

Evidence of Mithraic rites among the Romans are found mainly at Rome and Ostia, with substantial finds on the frontier of the empire, including Brittania, as well as along the Rhine and Danube rivers, and in Syria. Related swords found in Syria have what looks like the letter 'S' stamped into their blade.[25] While some scholars have argued that this might be a 'totemic symbol or tribal marking' that may represent a snake,[26] it is more likely that the marking is derived from *tamga*, symbols used by the Sarmatians to mark their belongings, including armour and livestock.

A consistent trait of Mithras is that he wears a Phrygian cap. This has led some scholars to suggest that he was originally a

Parthian god, but the dates do not work. Phrygian caps were also worn by other peoples, notably several steppe cultures including the Alano-Sarmatians, with whom the Romans came into contact in the first century BCE.

Antonia Triplites argued that Mithraism developed from the worship of Mitra in India and transmitted westward, acquiring details from other cultures on the way.[27] This expands on the hypothesis that Mithras was the premier god of the Iranian religion prior to the reforms of Zarathustra (Zoroaster in Greek) in the sixth century BCE. This is the old Indo-Iranian origin hypothesis that has long been disproven in favor of the Indo-European origin hypothesis. Mithraic worship was transmitted to the Crimea, possibly from Russia, in particular its southern steppes, rather than from Persia. The religion diffused, rather than being created by parallel development, reaching as far south as Numidia in north-west Africa. Parallels to the Indic Mitra include that Mithras was a god of contracts, but he was also a god of war, hence his popularity among the Roman legions.

In Plutarch's *Life of Pompey*, pirates in Cilicia, a Roman province on the south-east coast of what used to be Hittite territory, were worshiping Mithras in 68 BCE.[28] Plutarch also states that the pirates supported Mithridates VI, King of Pontus, which was north of Cilicia, in his war against the Roman Republic. At this time the religion may have passed from the pirates to the Persians. This supports Cumont's contested suggestion that the religion of Mithras came from Iran.[29] Where Cumont did not go was further back in time, to the Hittite sword god. Ulansey contended that Roman Mithraism used Hipparchus' 'discovery' of the precession of the equinoxes (*c.* 190–120 BCE; see chapter 9) as a foundation for the religion of Mithras. We contend that the story is much, much older and began with the nomads of the Eurasian steppes, coming from the same source as the Hittite sword god.

Like Ogun, whom we shall meet in chapter 6, Mithras uses a knife – or possibly a sword – to sacrifice animals. Most images show him slitting the throat of a bull. Given the celestial nature of the representations, it is generally assumed that the bull is Taurus. Many possible constellations have been proposed for Mithras, including Perseus. The Roman poet Statius (*c*. 80 CE) wrote of Mithras' cave in his epic poem *Thebaid*. Mithras battles with a horned creature in a 'Persian' cave. There seems to be something celestial going on here since, as J. H. Mozley pointed out, the word is *Persean*, not *Persian*. This would refer to the mythical ancestor of the Persians, Perses (Πέρσης), the son of Andromeda and Perseus, both of whom became constellations. (Andromeda also contains a galaxy by the same name.)[30] But neither the story of Perses nor that of Perseus matches the Mithraic tale. We suggest that the constellation Mithras represents is Aries, which we will discuss further in chapter 9. Whatever the case, the first-century Romans still knew something that later peoples forgot. The story of the embedded sword was tied up in the star lore and a change in the heavens. Mithras had a part to play in that.

The Story Transformed

In 1982 Scott Littleton demonstrated that sword heroes, as well as sword gods, are deeply rooted in the North Iranian epic tradition and that the Sword in the Stone episode, which plays such an important role in the Arthurian legends, was carried to western Europe by Sarmatians and Alans in the early centuries CE. We may recall that we encountered steppe nomads in Jason's tale of the Golden Fleece. Also, while Apollodorus of Athens did not write until the second century BCE, and Plutarch not until the first or second century CE, Theseus' story probably predates them by centuries. Given that we know the Hittites were carrying a similar tale that they probably took from north of the Black Sea, and that the ancestors of the Greeks came from the same region, it is more than possible that the Greeks acquired the seeds of this tale from the same locale. These tribes were part of the north-eastern Iranian-speaking Indo-European peoples who lived adjacent to the ancient Greeks, whose language also developed from the proto-Indo-European language as did the Hittite language. With such transmission of languages comes the transmission of stories, but the transmission of the Sword in the Stone story seems to be by diffusion rather than by parallel development given the dates and distribution of the tales.

In addition to a sword, a stone, a bull and a ram, another figure has appeared: a god associated with horses. Poseidon features in the stories of both Jason and Theseus, and while we know him best as the Greco-Roman god of the sea, Puhvel has suggested that this new god, associated with horses, earthquakes, and volcanoes, was slotted in above Okeanos, part of the original Greek substratum, sometime during the second millennium BCE, after the Hittites invaded Anatolia.[31] That substratum had conquered the indigenous peoples of Greece, and, judging by Poseidon's association with horses, they were in turn conquered by horse-riding peoples, most likely from the south Russian steppes. These were the ancestors of the People of the Sea, raiders who attacked Egypt and other Mediterranean locations possibly from Anatolia from 1200 to 900 BCE.[32]

At the same time, the war god Ares almost certainly came in from the steppes, either from Thrace or Anatolia, and we also continue the solar imagery with Helios and his golden, dragon-drawn chariot in the sky. As the story moves west, the dragons are replaced by horses, though the dragon motif remained in eastern variants of the tale for reasons that we will explore in chapter 9. At this point Apollo, another late arrival, takes over as the driver until the Romans come along and match the ancient Helios to their sun god, Sol.

The pieces are starting to come together, though their precise meaning is still unclear. The further we get from the original story, the more a succession of people forget why they are telling it and change some of the details. What was one tale for the Hittites is now two different narratives for the Greeks, and the war god Ares is now associated with the tale sufficiently to allow Herodotus to identify the sword god of the Scythians with the Greek Ares.[33] Yaggy and Haines describe a sword dance performed by three female jugglers among descendants of the steppe nomads, one of whom is depicted 'turning somersaults forwards and backwards across the points of three swords stuck in the ground'.[34] This inevitably recalls the bull-leaping performers of Crete in the Theseus tale, which we saw as connecting the bull, the sun god, and the underworld with the story of the sword bearer. Some pieces of information concerning a shift in the heavens and the moving of the sword from south to north were still being relayed – something important enough for people to keep passing the tale down through the ages. Yet before we explore how this may have happened, we need to turn to the most familiar of all the Sword in the Stone stories – that of King Arthur demonstrating his right to rule in Britain.

3

THE SWORDS OF ARTHURIAN TRADITION

The Sword in the Stone

Probably the most famous scene in Arthurian literature depicts the young Arthur pulling the sword from the stone. It is also the scene that is most frequently portrayed incorrectly. Robert de Boron originally wrote the tale of the young Arthur in his *Merlin* (*c.* 1200 CE). While much of his poem was inspired by Geoffrey of Monmouth's *Historia regum Britanniae* (*The History of the Kings of Britain*), which was written some seventy-five years earlier, Robert included something that Geoffrey did not: the story of the Sword in the Stone. Only 504 lines of this text have survived, but the poem was summarised in prose, so we know what Robert wrote. Essentially, following the death of Uther Pendragon, the kingdom of Logres (the Latinised name for England from the Welsh Lloegyr) is without a ruler. The lords of the country begin to quarrel over who will succeed him, and Merlin, who has been keeping an eye on things, arranges a test that will discover the rightful king.

While everyone was at Christmas Mass, a 'great square block of stone and an anvil appeared, and in the anvil was fixed a sword' in the courtyard of a church.[1] Everyone comes out of the cathedral and sees it. 'Then [the archbishop] noticed what was written on the sword: that whoever could draw the sword from the stone would be king by the choice of Jesus Christ.'[2]

But no one could draw it. A further tournament was held at Candlemas to see who should try again. Arthur, who is Uther's son, and brought up in ignorance of his true identity at Merlin's behest by Sir Entor (Ector), arrives on the scene to attend the tournament, serving as squire to his foster brother Kay. In the excitement of the gathering Arthur forgets Kay's sword at their lodging, but when he goes back for it there is no one there to let him in. '[O]n his way back he passed the church and took the sword that was fixed in the stone.'[3]

Kay claims to have pulled out the sword himself, but his father demands that he demonstrate this. When Kay cannot, he confesses that it was Arthur who did so. Entor gets the boy to show him and, when he succeeds, he tells the archbishop, who also demands a demonstration. When Arthur succeeds again, the archbishop embraces the boy and sings a *Te Deum Laudamus* (a hymn traditionally sung at times of celebration) over him. He then declares that according to the writing on the sword the boy must be the next king. Pandemonium ensues. Arthur is required to plunge the sword into the stone and take it out again several times, but despite this the barons of England are not satisfied: 'Whatever test this child may have passed, we know next to nothing about him.'[4] They then demand a further test at

Easter, and when this still does not enable anyone other than Arthur to draw the sword, there is yet a further delay until Pentecost. Here, at last, Arthur is accepted and duly crowned king. His true parentage is only then revealed, amid much rejoicing.

This story is present not only in Robert's *Merlin* (*c.* 1191–1202), but also in the *Didot-Perceval* (*c.* 1200), the *Queste del Saint Graal* (early thirteenth century), the *Prose Merlin* (mid-1200s, a redaction of Robert's work), and the *Coronacio Arthuri* (mid-fifteenth century) as well as what remains the best-known version, retold by Sir Thomas Malory in his *Le Morte d'Arthur*, published in 1485. Defined by Stith Thompson in the *Motif-Index of Folk Literature* as motif D1654.4.1 ('Sword can only be moved by right person') and motif H31.1 ('Recognition by unique ability to dislodge sword'), there seems to be more to this pattern than independent creation.

Later variants change a few of the details. Malory has it that:

> There was seen in the churchyard, against the high altar, a great stone four square, like unto a marble stone; and in midst thereof was like an anvil of steel a foot high, and therein stuck a fair sword naked by the point, and letters that were written in gold about the sword that said thus: 'Whoso pulleth out this sword of this stone and anvil is rightwise king born of all England.'[5]

During the delays following the initial miraculous events, a pavilion is erected over the stone and the sword, and ten knights – later reduced to five – are set to watch over it day and night.

Fig. 2. Medieval pavilion. (W. Kinghan)

The inference in Malory's version is clearly that Merlin rather than God is responsible for the miracle. But the other details, such as Arthur running for Kay's sword and taking the sword from the anvil (which comes and goes in some of the tales), remain the same. A feature that is equally consistent is that Arthur keeps plunging the sword into the stone and withdrawing it from the time he first draws it, near the beginning of the liturgical year, until Pentecost, which celebrated the day when the Holy Spirit reputedly descended upon Jesus' disciples. At that point the commoners demanded that Arthur should be crowned king. That satisfied all but eleven kings, who subsequently went to war with Arthur. Once he had beaten them, the Round Table was founded, and the main story gets underway.

There are two types of Arthurian writings dating from the Middle Ages. On the one hand, we have the Romances, lengthy tales of chivalry and love, most of which include the Sword in the Stone episode; on the other hand, we have Chronicles, beginning with Geoffrey of Monmouth, which lay claim to a more historical foundation (though they are more properly described as pseudo-history often written with propaganda in mind, which do not include the story of the Sword in the Stone.

That the story of the Sword in the Stone appears to originate from Continental sources seems clear enough. Although the native British (or Welsh) tales that refer to Arthur, such as 'Culhwch and Olwen', written down in the eleventh century, give Arthur a magical sword, they do not refer to any such test.[6] Malory explicitly described his source as 'the French book' – probably referring to the *Lancelot-Grail* cycle – and complained that it did not include parts of the tale, such as the name of the cathedral everyone was worshipping in when the sword appeared. Malory makes this Old St Paul's in London, while Robert's text says that the sword appeared in the city of Logres, which may or may not be on the Continent despite the Welsh connection to the name of the realm.

Fig. 3. Old St Paul's (Wikimedia Commons)

The tale is an odd one, and the form it takes in the two surviving versions of the text do not agree. The original manuscript of Malory's work vanished sometime in the period of fifteen years between his death in 1470 and its publication by William Caxton in 1485. The Winchester Manuscript, which only came to light in the 1920s, does little to enlighten Caxton's edition but is closer to Malory's original. The Winchester version has Arthur crowned as king of all Britain, not just of England. Sir Kay forgets his sword but remembers the sheath. There is no pavilion with watching knights. Arthur pulls the sword free without reading the inscription. What the two manuscripts do agree on is that the proposed site for the miracle was Old St Paul's in London. In contrast to Robert, Malory chose to set the action in London. He will almost certainly have read that Logres was a country ruled over by the legendary Brutus of Troy, who gave his name to the island of Britain, not just a city as Robert implies. Dissatisfied with this more obscure setting, Malory moved the action to the English capital.

Malory's choice of Old St Paul's is particularly interesting because of the church's unique architecture. In the story, there is much coming and going of high-ranking nobles between the interior of the church and the exterior, where the sword and stone appear against a second high altar. Old St Paul's had just such an outdoor pulpit that was part of a church built over a temple of the goddess Diana, dating back to the period of the Roman occupation.

Founded in 604 CE by Mellitus, a companion of St Augustine, the original building, which served as a gathering point for governmental activities, announcements of important news and other secular matters, was replaced by William the Conqueror after it burned down on 7 July 1086. The resulting building lasted until the 1600s, when most of it burned to the ground in the Great Fire of London.

The only church dedicated to St Paul on lands once governed by the Western Roman Empire, its bells rang to signal the people to assemble for the Folkmote, an assembly where the townspeople got together to conduct business. It took about 200 years to build, and it was crowned 'by a cross and a gilt pommel' set into the wooden structure.[7] In 1314 the cross and ball were replaced with another, following damage to the first. Relics were placed in the cross to protect the building from storms, including two stones: one from the Holy Sepulchre and one from the site of the Ascension. The Lady Chapel, dedicated to the Virgin Mary, who was honoured by both King Arthur and Sir Gawain, featured a rose window, not unlike the one that would grace the future Notre-Dame de Paris, the flower being intimately connected with the Virgin Mary as well as with the Roman goddess Flora, whose worship she overtook in the late second century CE. The gathering place for the people to discuss things such as who would become king was to the east of the cathedral, where the outdoor pulpit was located. In 1382 lightning struck the cross, which was rebuilt with 'stone steps ... strong oak, and ... roofed with lead'.[8]

So strong was the connection between Old St Paul's and Arthur that Prince Arthur (1486–1502), son of Henry VII and named after this famous 'ancestor', was married to Catharine of Aragon there on 14 November 1501, at the ripe old age of fifteen, five months before his mysterious death.

Most subsequent authors take their retelling from Malory's tale, but they drop a few important details. They rarely put the Sword in the Stone in a pavilion as Malory described it. By this he probably meant something similar to the circular tents used by knights (see Fig. 2), though it could represent the firmament as did Mithras' cloak. We shall encounter this circular structure again in our next chapter. The anvil tends to come and go in later tales, as does the four-square shape of the stone, both of which are important. The various authors rarely manage to remember that a churchyard is also a graveyard – or at least near a grave or graveyard – in this case near the high altar of Old St Paul's, where notable people were entombed. These are all things Malory would have known about the building, since he would have visited the cathedral frequently in his lifetime.

Little is made of the fact that the Sword in the Stone first appears on Christmas Day, when Arthur also draws the sword in Robert's account, while in Malory's version he repeatedly draws it for the benefit of the barons and to convince the people of his right to rule until Pentecost. Arthur thus spends the better part of the year plunging the sword back into the stone and pulling it out again at every major festival in the ecclesiastical calendar. As Malory has it:

> Therewithal they went unto the Archbishop, and told him how the sword was achieved, and by whom. And on the Twelfth-day all the barons came thither, and to assay to take the sword, who that would assay. But there afore them all, there might none take it out but Arthur ... And right as Arthur did at Christmas, he did at Candlemas, and pulled out the sword easily ... so did he at Easter ... And at the feast of Pentecost ... [A]nd Arthur forgave them, and took the sword between both his hands, and offered it upon the altar where the Archbishop was, and so was he made knight of the best man that was there.[9]

In other words, starting at Christmas until roughly forty days after Easter the kings and knights of Britain kept a twelve-year-old boy sticking a sword into and pulling it out of an anvil atop a stone until he placed it on an altar and picked it up from there. Finally, the majority of nobles stopped arguing about whether or not Arthur should be king, with the exception of eleven kings who did not agree and whom he had to defeat in battle. Eleven wars were won, and with the help of Merlin he established the Round Table, where no one man was more important than any other, to help keep the peace.

Note that in Christianity, unlike Christmas, Ash Wednesday, Easter and Pentecost are moveable feasts. Easter is calculated by the first Sunday after the first full moon after the vernal equinox. This is a complicated formula, with Ash Wednesday falling roughly forty days before Easter and Pentecost falling roughly forty days after it. In other words, the season during which Arthur is putting the sword into and pulling it out of the stone or the anvil on the stone is determined by something echoed by the movement of the stars.

Rather than establishing a pattern for the tale of the Sword in the Stone, Malory's variant serves as something of a conflated form of several variants – as indeed does his entire work, which is at times more of a compilation than a single novel. Here we have:

(1) An underaged hero
(2) Who pulls a sword from an anvil
(3) Which is set atop a stone
(4) In a churchyard (graveyard)
(5) To earn the right to do something special (become king)
(6) The hero must pull the sword multiple times in front of witnesses at high holy days until the miracle is accepted

(7) An older hero/knight is present and is the first to accept the miracle

(8) A young hero is present who falsely claims to be the hero who performed the feat

(9) The sword flashes and gleams like a star

The story was so popular that it appears in manuscripts that do not have exclusively Arthurian content.[10] For example, a Picard scribe of the North French school depicted Arthur drawing the sword from the stone and anvil.[11] The manuscript in which this appears contains parts of the *Lancelot-Grail* cycle, including the *Estoire del Saint Graal* and a *Merlin*. It is dated to *c.* 1290, post Robert de Boron. The image with the stone and anvil is found in the Merlin section and appears in the top register. In the bottom register, Arthur places the sword on the altar during his coronation. While produced by the same group of scribes throughout, non-Arthurian material is included. The youth of the clergy in the scene is also worthy of note.[12] Apparently, the tale appealed to a younger audience.

Galahad and the Sword in the Grave

Arthur was not the only one in Malory's tale, or in his sources, who pulled a sword from a stone. Galahad, the son of Lancelot, deputed to be the successful Grail Knight in the later accounts of the quest, also performed this miracle – with a few modifications. In this adventure the sword is placed in a floating stone by Merlin, which may be why many authors assume that the original sword was placed in the stone by the wizard rather than by God as the archbishop assumes in Robert de Boron's account.

Galahad's sword originally belonged to the hero Balin. It came into Merlin's possession after Balin used it to slay his unrecognised brother Balan in an earlier episode of the Arthurian epic. Merlin thrusts the sword into the stone after burying the fratricidal brothers, and sets it to float on a river. Note that in this retelling the stone is not in a graveyard, though it is associated with two graves and the blade is that of a dead man who used it to slay his brother – a serious sin even if Balin did not know the identity of his victim. The stone floats down the river to a lake near Camelot, where it is taken out and many knights attempt to remove the sword from its stony prison. All fail until Galahad, who is a full-grown man rather than a boy, tries his hand at the sword and succeeds, proving that he is supposed to undertake the quest for the Holy Grail. Having been informed by a hermit figure who substitutes for Merlin, Galahad already knew he would succeed and brought an empty scabbard with him, which is reminiscent of Sir Kay's empty scabbard.

Malory describes the scene thus:

King Arthur took Sir Galahad by the hand and led him to the lake to show him a stone which had risen from the depth of the waters. The stone appeared to float upon the water and in it was a bright sword with handles wrought with precious stones and gold. Upon the sword were written the words: 'Never shall man take me hence but only he by whose side I ought to hang, and he shall be the best knight of the world.' Arthur instructed Galahad to try and pull out the sword, after all the other knights had failed. And anon, he laid his hand on the sword, and lightly drew it out of the stone, and put it in the sheath.[13]

This part of the story was considered important enough to include among the carvings executed in the nineteenth century by Henry Hugh Armstead in the royal robing room within the

Palace of Westminster in London, where the reigning monarch robes up before entering Parliament.[14]

In a later MS, dated 1463 and dealing with the Tristan story, an artist of the French school depicted Galahad drawing the sword from the floating stone as Arthur looks on.[15] We know quite a bit about this manuscript. It was created for 'Eleanor de Bourbon, the Countess of La Marche ... and ... her son ... Jacques d'Armagnac, Duc de Nemours'.[16] It is dated precisely to 8 October 1463 and was penned by 'Micheay Gonnot de la Brouce, prestre, demourant a Crousant'.[17] The illuminations of Galahad are considered to be some of the finest in the entire 773-leaf manuscript.[18] The depiction of Arthur here is very similar to the Biblical figure of 'the aged Samuel' in the upper part of a miniature, ascribed to an immediate precursor of Gonnot, in the *Mer des histories*.[19] In the Bible Samuel is the character who anoints Saul as the first king of Israel so there is a sense here of divine power being bestowed on a new generation. The artist may also have known and been thinking of another story entirely, which, while it had nothing to do with Arthur, featured a Sword in the Stone story that is still regarded as closely similar to the main Arthurian version. This is the story of the Perilous Cemetery.

The Perilous Cemetery

The episodes featuring the Perilous Chapel and Cemetery appear several times in the Arthurian tradition, particularly in the stories of Lancelot and in episodes relating to other Grail Knights such as Gawain, Ector and Galahad. This is a creepy place where one or more knights must confront a set of wonders that have more in common with Dante's *Inferno* than they do with the Knights of the Round Table.

Malory's tale is suitably macabre. Here Lancelot finds himself in an ancient castle, where he sees the body of a wounded knight. A lady then appears, weeping and wringing her hands, and begs him to go to the nearby Perilous Chapel and acquire a piece of bloody cloth that he will find wrapped around a sword. This alone will heal the wounds of the knight, who is her brother. Lancelot sets off:

> ... but when he came unto the Chapel Perilous he alighted down, and tied his horse unto a little gate. And as soon as he was within the churchyard he saw on the front of the Chapel many fair rich shields turned upside down, and many of the shields Lancelot had seen knights bare beforehand. With that he saw by him there stand as thirty great knights, more [tall] by a yard than any man that ever he had seen, and all those grinned and gnashed at Sir Lancelot. And when he saw their countenance he dreaded him sore, and so put his shield afore him and took his sword ready in his hand ready unto battle, and they were all armed in black harness ready with their shields and their swords drawn. And when Sir Lancelot would have gone throughout them, they scattered on every side of him, and gave him the way, and therewith he waxed all bold, and entered into the Chapel, and then he saw no lights but a dim lamp burning, and then he was aware of a corpse hild [wrapped] with a cloth of silk. Then Sir Lancelot stopped down, and cut away a piece of that cloth, and then it fared under him as the earth had quaked a little; therewithal he feared. And then he saw a fair sword lie by the dead knight, and that he got in his hand and hied him out of the Chapel.[20]

Once he leaves the chapel, Lancelot encounters a sorceress who tries to make him give up the sword. He refuses, and the sorceress confesses that had he done so she would have had power over him and been able to make him love her and that he would never have seen Queen Guinevere again. He then finds his way back to the castle and heals the knight by touching his wounds with the sword and wiping them with the bloody cloth. All of this has elements borrowed from the Grail myths, where the spear that wounds the Maimed King is the only thing that can heal him, while the bloody cloth reminds one of the both the *vesica* of Veronica, which is said to have borne the face of Christ, and the notorious blood-stained shroud of Turin, in which the body of Christ was supposedly buried.

The Perilous Chapel is usually surrounded by a wall that may or may not have the severed heads or shields of dead knights or something else unpleasant affixed to it. Inside is a graveyard. Here there can be anywhere from one to twelve graves with swords, planted hilt first in the middle of a fire. If there are twelve graves, the occupants are said to be the brothers of the companion of Joseph of Arimathea named Alain, the Fisher King. When the swords and fire are absent, up to thirty knights, dressed in black and as pleasant as the Grim Reaper, line the path to the chapel door as in the version above. They repeatedly demand that whichever knight is approaching should turn back. If the black knights are not along a path outside, they line the central aisle that leads to the high altar. Here, as we saw, Lancelot finds a dead knight – if the dead knight has not already appeared in one of the graves outside the chapel – wrapped in a shroud with a magical sword lying at his side on the altar. This is not unlike the way Arthur placed the sword from the stone on the high altar at Old St Paul's.

In variants of the above story the Arthurian knight gets to the chapel first, turns back and heads into a forest where the maiden tells him that she needs the sword and a piece of the shroud to cure her mortally wounded brother. The intrepid champion then makes the decision to re-enter the chapel, take the sword from the altar, and cut a piece of cloth from the shroud. The black knights try to stop him from leaving, but he prevails and returns to the maiden. He touches the sword to the brother's wound and uses the piece of the shroud as a bandage. The brother is healed, all three celebrate, and the knight leaves, though whether with or without the sword from the altar is uncertain. For instance, a similar story, featuring Sir Gawain, appears in the thirteenth-century French romance *L'âtre Perilleus* (*The Perilous Cemetery*).

Not every story in Arthurian the romances matches the quality of the illuminations in the 1463 manuscript, but several artists seem to have had a particular fondness for illustrating 'strange perils',[21] and this was certainly one of them. An illuminator of the North French school depicted the scene in the Perilous Cemetery in a manuscript of the *Lancelot*, dated *c.* 1300–1320 CE.[22] Once again we have the tombs of the twelve brothers, all surrounded by fire, and with their swords positioned hilt down on top of them. As Hector/Ector and Gawain, in this version, approach, the blades attack them while the wielders remain invisible.

Here again we have that number twelve, recalling the warriors on the Hittite cave at Yazılıkaya and the Twelve Companions who appear in several of the older myths, long before the time of Arthur.

Military tactics, arms, armour and stories were not the only thing to spread from the Continent to Britain. Alain, whose name is featured in the story of the Fisher King, is another spelling for the name Alan. The Alans invaded Roman Gaul in the early fifth century, settling in areas such as northern Gaul and Armorica

(Brittany), which gave rise to some of the Grail legends, as well as in southern Gaul, which added the stories of the Maimed King and the Fisher King, both guardians of the sacred vessel. While the Scythians were known to stick swords into *kurgans*, possibly lighting fires atop the burials as well, their cousins the Alans took to diverting rivers, burying their fallen leaders with treasure in the riverbed, and then returning the river to its normal course. This may be why we have stories of heroes being born beside rivers. But how do we explain the fires on the graves and the information that the Fisher King's name is Alain, things that seem to transmit without the audience knowing why? One clue to this may lie in the story of Lancelot's search for his origins.

At first glance this tale of Sir Lancelot does not appear to be an embedded-sword story, though Lancelot does remove a sword with healing properties from the altar – properties akin to those conferred on Excalibur by the magical scabbard given to Arthur by the Lady of the Lake. As Littleton and Malcor noted in *From Scythia to Camelot*,[23] there are certain patterns to the way Arthur and Lancelot acquire their weapons that seem to parallel each other. Arthur pulls his first sword from an anvil atop a stone and receives his second sword as a gift from the Lady of the Lake. Lancelot receives his first sword from the Lady of the Lake and acquires his second sword in a manner that we want to examine in some detail at this point.

Ulrich von Zatzikhoven, author of the twelfth-century story of *Lanzelet*, apparently knew the tradition that Lancelot had two swords, although he does not relate the precise scene where the hero picks up the second sword. What Ulrich does do is describe the Lady of the Lake (the Queen of the Sea) as 'the gracious queen who had reared him and taught him virtue, taken pains with him and given him his first sword'.[24]

Sometimes the pieces of this story are present without the sword. For instance, in Chrétien de Troyes' *Le Chevalier du Chariot* (*The Knight of the Cart*) there is a scene where Lancelot visits a cemetery and lifts the stone slab from atop a tomb to prove that he is the knight who is destined to 'free all the men and women who are imprisoned in the land'.[25] When Lancelot completes this quest in the prose *Lancelot*,[26] all the graves in the graveyard and the helmets that had adorned the crenels of the castle (the heads had been displayed while the bodies had been buried) disappear. Although there are also literal prisoners freed in the medieval texts, what we may have here is an ancient tale about the raising of the dead.

The great knight knows nothing of his parentage, having been raised by the Lady of the Lake. In search of his true lineage, he arrives at the familiar haunted chapel/graveyard. Once again, this does not immediately appear to be an embedded-sword story; indeed, Lancelot appears to be more worried about the black knights with their zombie-like smiles, upside-down shields, an earthquake and the creepy sorceress to give much thought to embedded swords. What he does succeed in doing is pulling a sword off an altar, a blade that possesses healing powers akin to those of Excalibur's scabbard, which Arthur received from the Lady of the Lake.

The following story, from the thirteenth-century romance of *Perlesvaus*, adds another layer to the version above, in which a crossbow bolt is buried in a pillar, which, however, takes Lancelot to the Perilous Chapel.[27] In this episode a jewelled and golden crossbow bolt appears suddenly embedded in a pillar during the feast of Pentecost while Arthur and his court are at Carduil (Carlisle). Both Gawain and Lancelot declared it was the finest they had ever seen – though most of it was hidden in the pillar, so powerful was its trajectory. As the court are still looking on in wonder a maiden appears on a beautiful mule. She begs Arthur to send a knight who can withdraw the bolt from the pillar to a place where he is much needed. Lancelot immediately rises and with great force pulls it out and hands it to the maiden. Weeping, the maiden tells him he must go the Perilous Chapel where he will find a knight lying in a tomb. Lancelot is instructed to take part of the shroud that covers the dead knight and a sword that lies beside him. He carries out these instructions and gives the sword and cloth to the maiden, and the cloth is later used to heal a wounded knight. The same story appears in a truncated form in *Le Morte d'Arthur*.

So here we have Lancelot pulling a weapon from a pillar to prove his right to undertake a quest. This is something we will discuss further in chapter 9, when the hero pulls the sword from (or embeds the sword in) a tree or pillar rather than a stone.

Arthur and Arcturus

Long before this episode, or that of the Sword in the Stone, Arthur had his own associations with star lore – based around his name *Artos*, which means Bear. This led an identification with the star of Arcturus (the Great Bear) from at least as early as the twelfth century. Here, perhaps we are back in the same territory we were with Kallisto in ancient Greece.

A further detail which often passes unnoticed in the consideration of Arthur's sword is the fact that, as Malory puts it, the blade 'was so bright in his enemies' eyes that it gave the light of thirty torches'. This suggests an almost starlike aura to the sword, and may be a part of the material that places Arthur in the heavens. We shall explore this further in Appendix 1 – for the moment it is enough to say that the astrological connection between Arthur and the story of the heavens is very much a part of our argument.

Wulfstan

These highly wrought medieval romances were not the only place in which we hear a distant echo of the Sword in the Stone motif at this time. As noted, one of the details that recurs frequently in the embedded-sword theme is that the blade is planted in a graveyard, or at least in a grave or altar. Just in case there is any doubt of that, variants exist with other weapons that leave no room for doubt. One such tale is that of a knight named Wulfstan. According to *Edwardis regis Anglorum*,[28] finished in 1138 by Osbert de Clare, when Wulfstan's colleagues were disputing his right to hold his office, he verified that King Edward the Confessor had appointed him by plunging his staff into the king's tomb, which is in Westminster Abbey, and demonstrating that he was the only man who could withdraw it. Wulfstan's story also apparently echoed an earlier tale, told about another Wulfstan, an archbishop, who accidentally stabbed his staff between the flagstones of a monastery. Here again we have the combination of stabbing and withdrawing a sword or, in this case, a staff.

The story was well known during the reign of Henry II, where noble audiences could not help comparing it to the tale of Arthur's Sword in the Stone, given that the Arthurian tradition was so favoured by the king's wife, Eleanor of Aquitaine, and that his second son, Richard Lionheart, was said to carry Arthur's sword Excalibur. It is interesting, though, that the Wulfstan story is associated with the reign of King John rather than with Richard's, Wulfstan being John's patron saint. John carried Tristan's sword rather than Arthur's,[29] and that sword was used by Arthur's knight to swear his oath to King Mark by placing it on an altar, a custom practised by medieval knights. So here we have King John connected with a staff in a grave and/or stone along with a sword on an altar.

Another tradition which seems to have been brought into play in the sixteenth century, and which is based in London, is that of the Sword Rests, which were to be found in every church throughout the city. These were originally stones, but later migrated to wood or metal racks which the Lord Mayor of the city, who visited a different church every week during his time in office, commanded his sword bearer to lay his sword of state in or upon when entering. The sword was generally placed in an upright position, so that it must have been strikingly similar in appearance to the sword placed in the stone by Merlin. The tradition ceased in 1883 but a number of these sword rests have survived until the present time. The wrought iron frames can be as tall as 6 feet and include both the royal arms and those of the current Lord Mayor. These latter examples are built around a central pole, which may remind one of the pole of the heavens, though this is almost certainly coincidental. The existence of these curious objects seems to chime with the presence of the Sword in the Stone in St Paul's and is typical of the way in which ancient customs and symbols remain even when their origins may be forgotten.[30]

Though these instances may seem like a high point of the journey of the Sword in the Stone motif – and certainly are forever associated with Arthur and his knights – there are other intriguing tales from the medieval period that show just how important the theme was to the medieval world and in how many strange ways it made its appearance. One such is the story of the twelfth-century saint Galgano, which we will explore next.

4

GALGANO'S EMBEDDED SWORD

One of the lesser-known stories of the Sword in the Stone that academics have repeatedly tried to connect with that of King Arthur is the tale of St Galgano. Supposedly born in 1148 at Chiusdino (not far from Siena), Galgano was the son of Guidotto Guidotti and a certain Dionigia. As such stories go, he was a young wastrel, and the situation only got worse after his father died. Enter the Archangel Michael, of whom Galgano has a vision where the Archangel tells Dionigia to have Galgano become a holy knight. Then Michael walks away, and Galgano sees himself following the Archangel.

Instead of going to war in the name of God, since Galgano was only an infant at the time of the Second Crusade, Galgano began to follow a life of penitence. A frustrated Michael appeared again, this time telling Galgano to climb Montesiepi, a mountain fairly close to the knight's home, and live his humble life there instead of in the safety of his mother's house.

Galgano told his mother of the vision, and she promptly became hysterical because he was his deceased father's only heir and she needed him to inherit the property and take care of her. For this reason Galgano's family decided to marry him off so he could at least sire an heir before going into seclusion.

About 20 miles from Chiusdino lived a very wealthy man by the name of Antonnio Brizzi in a grand castle at Civitella Marittima. He had a beautiful daughter named Polissena who was to be Galgano's bride and his mother's hope of keeping Galgano from Montesiepi. Galgano resisted his family's intentions for a long time but eventually agreed to see Polissena, forgetting the calling of the Archangel.

Galgano set out for Civitella Marittima when, about 4 miles from Chiusdino, in the plain of Morella, his horse suddenly stopped and refused to go any further. Galgano dismounted and fell to his knees. Recognising his failure, he pleaded for forgiveness when the Archangel Michael appeared to him yet again and commanded that he follow him to Montesiepi, where he should do harsh penance. From that moment on Galgano was enrolled in the army of Heaven. In the vision the Archangel guided him along a narrow and difficult path to Montesiepi.

At the top of the mountain Galgano found a circular temple, and there he met the Twelve Apostles. Stunned, Galgano exclaimed that a sinner such as he should not be granted so blessed a vision, saying that it would be easier for him to plunge his sword into a stone than to be forgiven. He then proceeded to do just that, plunging his sword into the stony ground, leaving just the cross-shaped hilt in view. This supposedly happened on 1 December 1180, nine years before the Third Crusade.

Instead of finding a temple, in some variants Galgano built 'a circular hut ... of branches' around the sword, which he used as his cross.[1] This recalls immediately the sword in the anvil in the circular tent described by Malory. Following a fairly standard encounter with the Devil, and in spite of a command from a heavenly voice (presumably St. Michael's) never to leave the site, Galgano journeyed to Rome, apparently because his disciples irritated him. He went to seven Roman churches and then to Pope Alexander III (r. 1159–1181), but no one had a solution for him.[2]

While he was gone, three vandals attempted to destroy the hut and sword. Later variants identify these three men as assassins. They broke the hilt off the sword and fled. One man drowned, one was struck by lightning, and the third had his arms chewed off by wolves, a traditional folkloric triple death spread over three individuals rather than all happening to one person.[3] When Galgano returned from Rome, he was despondent over the broken sword. The heavenly voice told him to place the hilt against the blade. Galgano obeyed, and the sword became whole again. The vandal who was attacked by wolves returned to beg Galgano's forgiveness and became one of Galgano's followers. Galgano prayed with his disciples for almost a year, but when two bishops came to pray with him on 3 December 1181, they found him dead in the hut.[4] The bishops and the abbots of Fossanova attended Galgano's funeral,[5] burying him somewhere near the sword. There's that Sword in the Stone in the graveyard tale again, this time with severed arms as well, something we will encounter in chapter 5.

Later authors provide Galgano with an already established fiancé instead of a newly proposed one as an excuse for his journey over the mountain.[6] Whatever the case, there is general agreement that on a visit to Civitella, Galgano found Montesiepi.[7] In these later versions, on reaching the top,

Galgano plunged his sword into the rocky ground and took up residence, slitting his cloak to use as a monk's cowl.[8] Some variants give the date for this as 21 December 1180, the winter solstice.

Following his death, Galgano was quickly canonised. The canonisation is very odd. There is no contemporary record of any canonisation trial, such as would normally happen in such a situation in order to judge whether Galgano was a suitable candidate for sainthood.[9] Although William of Malavalle predeceased him by about thirty years, it takes Galgano only four years to be canonised, while William (who has essentially the same story, minus the Sword in the Stone) is not canonised until much later, even though he founded an order of monks – the barefoot friars, who eventually became Augustinians. Roland of Pisa gives 1185 as the date.[10] Some tales credit Emperor Frederick Barbarossa with putting in a word on Galgano's behalf during the canonisation trial. Many more important saints (e.g. Augustine) in addition to William took far longer to be canonised. Galgano's fast-track may have something to do with Frederick being one of the leaders of the Third Crusade, Galgano's life overlapping his reign, and Galgano's association with Crusaders.

The story of the three vandals is based on a classic folktale, best known in its form of the threefold death. It is an Indo-European story in which someone, usually a hero or king, dies three ways at the same time: by hanging (or falling) from a tree, by being wounded, and by being drowned. In this variant, each of the modes of death is assigned to a different individual. The death by lightning and by drowning are classical features of this story, representing the hero as warrior and the hero as fertility figure. The death by hanging, the one that represents the hero as priest, is replaced in Galgano's tale by having one's arms torn off by wolves. It is this odd third 'death' that dominates, since this is the death used when the tale is told of only one vandal. Even in later variants of thieves who attempt to pull the sword out of the stone, the detail about arms being pulled off remains. It is apparent from this that there are some older elements to the legend – one that was considered to be an essential part of the story of Galgano by the local populace, though the people who told it clearly no longer had any idea why.

As we noted earlier, the story of the threefold death is also part of the Merlin story, as told by Geoffrey in Monmouth in the twelfth-century *Vita Merlini*.[11] In this Merlin foretells the death of a boy in three different ways, and only later is it discovered that the boy in question did indeed die by falling from his horse and hanging upside down from a branch with his head beneath the water of a river. This has been considered a type of Druidic ritual, and bodies have been discovered in Britain and Ireland which show signs of having been struck on the head, garrotted and drowned.[12]

A curious reference, dating from around 1303, comes from an early version of the *Prophecies of Merlin*. This is the first and oldest surviving version of what became almost a production line of prophetic books attributed to Merlin among others. The quotation here is from an edition of 1486, and, while the reference is slight, it not only points to the knowledge of the saint's story but also associates it with the figure of Merlin. The reference comes in a sequence where Merlin describes the presence of serpents or dragons which represent, in this context, the Antichrist. The mention of Galgano's Sword in the Stone is interesting as it talks of a 'serpent stone' in which the sword is embedded. Since serpent stones, within the context of the Prophecies, represent evil, this suggests that in thrusting his sword into the earth Galgano was defeating the works of the Antichrist.

> One day, Merlin was summoned by King Uther Pendragon. He asked Merlin: 'How did the dragons of Vortigern's tower live underground? Merlin said: 'Come with me:' He led the King to the valley where there was a round block of stone, without locks or wire mesh, and therefore completely closed. Merlin said: 'A small snake is trapped in this stone and is gnawing at it.' Uther Pendragon gave an order for the stone to be split. The snake flew out and Merlin caught it and showed how sharp its teeth were. Then Merlin said: 'These teeth are sharp enough to gnaw their way into the stone. They can fly over the earth and cause harm to everyone, people and animals.' Then Merlin added: 'There is a sword in the serpent-stone at Monte Gargano, and from the mountain no one can take it out except the chosen one.'[13]

This connection between the Sword in the Stone and serpents/dragons will be discussed in Chapter 8, when the story reappears in Japan.

The Site

There is nothing but sand and gravel under Galgano's stone, yet the stone itself is of a type commonly found in the Apennine Mountains.[14] The stone has a fissure in it into which any of a number of swords could have fit over the centuries. Analysis of nearby slag from the ironworks overseen by the Cistercians shows that the trace metals for the sword and slag do not match, so the current sword came from somewhere other than the location where Galgano would most likely have obtained his weapon.[15] The leading expert on the Galgano story, Luigi Garlaschelli, speculates that the sword may be a medieval fake put in the stone by the Cistercians after they took over the site.[16] Garlaschelli interviewed an eyewitness who said that in the early 1920s the sword was able to be pulled out of and pushed back into the fissure in the stone. In 1924 someone poured molten lead into the crack, fixing the sword in place, which is why the blade broke when someone tried to pull it out of the stone in the 1960s. This act of vandalism was apparently repeated in 1991, and the sword was once more secured in place, this time with concrete.

Galgano's body was exhumed a year or so after his death, and his blond hair had continued to grow.[17] His head was placed in a reliquary in a niche in the chapel, and his body was reinterred.[18] A pair of mummified forearms and hands, either from the vandal who was attacked by wolves or from a thief who tried to pull the Sword from the Stone and was hit by lightning, was exhibited in a second niche.[19]

The two mummified forearms are probably from the same individual.[20] What is more important, though, is that they are always said to be from 'enemies'. This detail calls to mind Herodotus' account of the Scythian sword god, who was offered the arms and hands of certain prisoners who were captured in war (see chapter 5). There is no textual relationship between Galgano's site and the Scythians, but a mitochondrial DNA study turned up a long history of similarity with Caucasian populations. Rudolf Arbesmann, an expert in saints' lives, also wrote that 'carbon-dating confirmed that two these mummified hands in the same chapel at Montesiepi were also from the twelfth century'.[21]

There is a rectangular mass in the floor near the sword which Garlaschelli thinks may be a grave, possibly the missing grave of Galgano himself. The mass has an east-west orientation, which is consistent with Christian burial. The orientation also matches that used by early steppe tribes, such as the 'classical' Sarmatians, whom we will discuss in chapter 5.

The Source of the Legend

The earliest form of Galgano's *Vita* is found in three manuscripts. Two are in the Biblioteca Comunale of Siena.[22] The third (MS Cod. Plut. 90 sup. 48) is in the Biblioteca Medicea Laurenziana of Florence. The first Siena manuscript is a seventeenth-century copy of one dating from the fourteenth century, penned by an anonymous Augustinian scribe. The second Siena manuscript contains a fourteenth-century copy of the *Vita* by Friar Roland of Pisa, who wrote *c.* 1220 CE,[23] and includes tales of miracles that happened after Galgano's death. That Roland is a 'friar' indicates that he was probably either a Franciscan or a Dominican, and given the number of Franciscan elements in Roland's variant he most likely belonged to that order. The version of Galgano's legend presented above is a compilation of all three *Vitae*.

The two fourteenth-century manuscripts date to the early part of that century, according to Uberto Benvolienti.[24] Several hundred other variants of Galgano's *Vita* exist, resulting from an ongoing debate between the Cistercians and the Augustinians as to which order can rightfully claim the saint.[25] The two bishops who discovered Galgano's body likely earned their place in the tale because of the ongoing battle among the various dioceses in the region as to which one could claim Galgano as their own.[26] St Francis was born in 1181, the year that Galgano supposedly died, which probably explains their interest.

Even though the earliest variants of the legend appear to be Augustinian and Franciscan, the Cistercians were actually the first order to claim the site, according to several historical documents.[27] This happened in 1201, after they reportedly built the round chapel, which became a very profitable pilgrimage destination.[28]

The documents include a *privilegium protectionis*, granted by Emperor Henry VI on 8 March 1191, Duke Philip of Tuscany's 26 February 1196 confirmation of the privileges granted to the monks by Frederick Barbarossa and Henry VI, a private deed of donation dated to 23 April 1196, and a mention of a certain Bonus as 'prior of the hermitage of San Galgano' in a document dated 6 October 1196.[29] Arbesmann concluded from this evidence that someone besides the Cistercians was already in possession of the Montesiepi chapel and that the Cistercians claimed it from them. The document that makes Bonus a Frenchman is a late forgery. It was not until 1206 that Innocent III agreed that the Cistercians were in charge of the site. The great abbey (built well after the chapel) contains Templar symbolism, which has led Garlaschelli to consider the possibility the Templars had something to do with the site, the care of which has always been attributed to the Cistercians. (There was a strong connection between the Templars and the Cistercians because both orders were founded by Bernard of Clairvaux.) As Garlaschelli points out,[30] it seems unlikely that Galgano himself was the connection;

there certainly isn't any evidence anywhere in the legend that he was a Templar, though the stories do suggest that he was intended to be a Crusader under Frederick Barbarossa.

In addition to the texts, there are the physical relics associated with Galgano. These include the forearms and hands, the head, and the Sword in the Stone. The hands and sword have been dated to the twelfth century. The reliquary for the head dates to the thirteenth century, well after the head was supposedly removed from the body, but the head itself has not been dated.[31] Pictorial evidence of the legend also exists in the form of frescoes, which Ambrogio Lorenzetti produced in 1340 in the side chapel on the north side of the rotunda. These show scenes from the life of Galgano, adding nothing to what the texts tell us.

Behind the Legend

Very little in the Galgano legend can actually be traced to fact. Montesiepi had a reputation as a ritual site, with the Etruscans receiving credit as the people who originally held religious services there. The non-Indo-European Etruscan language and Tuscan culture 'suddenly appear on the west coast of Etruria about 850 BCE',[32] and they seem to have had notable trade with Aegean Greeks as well as others, whose variant of the Sword in the Stone we considered in chapter 2. There may have been a priestly warrior caste of overlords among the Etruscans,[33] similar to what we see in Indo-European cultures, but historian Michael Grant thinks the culture was spread through trading contacts as people acquired Etruscan metal.[34] This fits nicely with our notion that the legend of the Sword in the Stone spread along with the knowledge of forging iron. The culture started along the coast (Populonia, Vetulonia and Corneto/Tarquinia) and moved inland to Chiusi and Perusia,[35] possibly carrying a variant of the Sword in the Stone. The culture was semi-Middle Eastern and had been present between Hellespont and north Syria at some point in time, representing invaders from Asia Minor.[36]

Some scholars have argued that Galgano's sword and the importance of the site as a pilgrimage destination led to the creation of the Sword in the Stone legend in the Arthurian tradition. Although Moiraghi's *The Enigma of St Galgano* is usually cited in articles that compare the Galgano legend to the Arthurian tale of the Sword in the Stone,[37] Luigi Garlaschelli's research into the relic had already been picked up by the press by 2001.

Recently there have been a number of attempts to derive the name Galgano from the Arthurian name Gawain. There is a 'Melconde Galganu' in the Life of St Kentigern,[38] a name that the Celticist Kenneth Hurlstone Jackson attempts to explain as a corruption of *Deganui* – after converting the name to de Galganu.[39] The hypothesis, presented by several Italian scholars, was that the Galgano legend supplied Robert de Boron with the source for his version of the tale. The linguistic argument is convoluted, however, and does not fit the timeline for the development of the Galgano tradition. Instead, a more likely explanation is that Galgano was named after the Aramaic *galgal*, 'wheel' (often translated into English as 'heaven' or 'whirlwind'). In this case, we could be looking at 'The Wheel God' or 'The Heavenly God', which could imply that Galgano's story originally belonged to the Christian god, though it could just as easily have belonged to some local, perhaps Indo-European, deity. Curiously, though, we once again find ourselves in a circle in the sky.

While the tales of Galgano and Arthur do share some key elements, there are also several major differences. Galgano plants his sword to give up war; Arthur removes the sword to wage war. Galgano is a full-grown man when his story takes place, not the underaged hero of the Arthurian variant. Galgano is a notorious sinner; Arthur is an innocent. There are no knights or other characters bearing Arthurian names in Galgano's tale, and there are no wolves, thieves who lose their hands while attempting to withdraw the sword or round chapels in the Arthurian account (though there is, of course, the roundish pavilion referred to in chapter 3). Galgano's success at mending the broken sword does reappear as a tale in the Arthurian tradition, but there it is told of Perceval as part of the Grail cycle and has nothing to do with Arthur and his Sword in the Stone. (Arthur does break the Sword in the Stone and, after placing the pieces in a lake, receives Excalibur from the Dame du Lac.) The differences between the tales are too numerous to list them all here, but this sampling should be enough to show that these narratives simply do not represent the mother–daughter relationship that would exist if Galgano's story had inspired Arthur's or vice versa. Instead, they show the development that would have incorporated different stories into the basic narrative as the tales were transmitted across cultures.

There is little to confirm the details of Galgano's life. The date of his birth seems to have been calculated backward from his reported death, based on the tradition that he was thirty-two or thirty-three years old at the time of his demise. No month or date is associated with Galgano's birth in any of the tales. Cardini places the date in 1147 instead of 1148, apparently because he thinks Galgano had a December birthday and could not yet have turned thirty-three if he was born in 1148 because he died no later than 3 December.[40] Galgano's age at the time of his death is also suspicious, since thirty-two is the age often stated as the age of Jesus when he died.

Galgano's family achieved nobility only in later texts.[41] The three earliest *Vitae* all describe the family as burghers.[42] In the Renaissance, the family is comprised largely of merchants. Despite assertions that 'Count' Guidotti was a Tuscan noble, the line of the Canossa counts of Tuscany ended with Mathilde in 1115, when she died and left her lands to the Pope. The Guidotti did eventually acquire part of Mathilde's holdings, granted to her by Frederick Barbarossa in 1160, when the House of Este presented them with the Palazzo Guidotti in 1676.[43] The Medici family ruled the area starting in 1197. In between those dates, Frederick Barbarossa held sway in the region. In 1160 he apparently gave a deed to the Palazzo Guidotti to a member of the Guidotti family, but that appears to be in the Reggio Emilia, to the north of Tuscany. Galgano's social promotion probably resulted from his vision of being dressed as a knight. If he was a knight, a storyteller may have reasoned, his family must have been noble.

The variants of Galgano's legend that present Guido and Dionigia as a childless older couple seem to have been largely modelled off the Biblical tale of Abraham and Sarah.[44] In short, there is no evidence that Galgano's parents ever existed. The earliest texts identify Guido as 'Guidocci', a diminutive of 'Guido'. A linguistic shift in thirteenth-century Pisa, when and where Roland wrote the earliest text, caused 'Guidocci' to be rendered as 'Guidocti'. From there it was a short step to equate 'Guidocti' with the well-known 'Guidotti' family. Galgano's mother, Dionigia, is equally suspicious. She is not assigned a family, and she does not appear in any records outside of Galgano's tale. Dionigia's name is the feminine form of Dionysius, a Thracian deity who was introduced into the Greek pantheon and later transferred to the Roman one.[45] He was a fertility god who was somehow connected with the Thracian Ares, and while there do not seem to be any fertility rites going on at the Galgano site, a sword god, rather than a fertility god, definitely seems to have been worshipped on the hilltop. In other words, the original Galgano probably had nothing at all to do with the Guidottis. Galgano's father, Guido Guidotti, does not have any existence outside of his son's legend.[46]

Galgano's fiancé, Polissena of Civitella Marittima, may also be a literary creation. The name Polissena is the medieval Italian form of the Greek Polyxena. In post-Homeric tradition, Polyxena was the sister of the ill-fated Trojan prophetess Kassandra. This story is from the *Ilioupersis*, *c.* 776–774 BC.[47] After the fall of Troy, Achilles' ghost demanded Polyxena as 'his share of the spoils',[48] so her throat was cut on his grave, enabling her to follow her master to Hades. Here, then, we have a tale of human sacrifice associated with the site, and this time it is a sacrifice to a warrior by the victim's throat being slit.

This all suggests that the Galgano story came from a tale that was extant before the story broke in two in the Greek culture. Perhaps it was carried to Magna Graecia in Italy around the eighth century BCE only to reemerge in the Middle Ages.

Galgano's tale features details from stories about at least three different Williams. There is William IX of Aquitaine, who was the uncle of William X, father of Eleanor of Aquitaine, who vanished during a pilgrimage, which led some biographers of William of Malavalle to scramble the Crusader with the Tuscan hermit. William of Malavalle's story may also be the source of the tale of the round chapel being built as Galgano's tomb, since the Williamites did indeed raise a chapel over William's grave.[49]

Tales that Galgano built a circular hut of branches on the site, starting construction on 21 December 1180, are definitely concocted. The round chapel has been dated to *c.* 985 CE.[50] There may have been a round structure made of branches on the site prior to the construction of the chapel, but Galgano did not put it there, nor did the Cistercians build the chapel on the site of Galgano's hut. The description of Galgano's hut does, however, match that of the Etruscan round huts made of branches found in Rome, which have been dated to the eighth century BCE, prior to the arrival of the Greeks, and the site has a reputation as a former centre of Etruscan worship.[51] Note the date, which coincides with the possible transmission of the tale from Greece. Some scholars have suggested that the round chapel was inspired by ancient Etruscan tombs. In this case, the round chapel was indeed thought to be Galgano's tomb,[52] but if the chapel originally contained a body, it was built for someone other than Galgano, someone who lived roughly two centuries before the saint.[53] It may also have given rise to another Arthurian theme, the supposedly circular 'Church of Wattles' built by Joseph of Arimathea in Glastonbury in the English county of Somerset to house the Holy Grail.

The feasts of many saints are held on days that formerly honoured pagan deities in an attempt to Christianise them. Galgano's feast was 3 December 1181.[54] This date was also the ancient Roman festival of the *Bona Dea*, the Roman 'Good Goddess', Fauna. Her festival was presided over by the Vestal Virgins, and men were barred from the ceremony. That fits with the design of the circular hut and the Etruscan connection, but it does not fit at all with the Sword in the Stone cult at the site. The Faunalia, which was held in honour of the shepherds' god Faunus, fell on 5 December. It's possible that the dates for the two festivals became blurred in the centuries after Rome's fall because Faunus is associated with some elements that do appear in Galgano's legend. For instance, the shepherds who worshipped Faunus built round huts out of branches, like Galgano's hut. The dance done at the Faunalia was also performed by the twelve Salii, priests of Mars Gradivus.[55] This was the warrior face of Mars, and the Salian worship was thought to descend from the Etruscans. Some scholars have equated Faunus with Lupercus, who used wolves to carry out his wishes. Lupercus, like Heracles, performed twelve labours, but his tasks very precisely match the constellations of the Zodiac. He also crossed the sky to collect the souls of the dead.[56]

The date on which Galgano supposedly built his hut suggests that the story was told to coincide with a specific festival that already existed. From about 200 CE onward, 21 December was the feast of St Thomas the Apostle (Doubting Thomas). The day may have been chosen to reflect something about Galgano's character. It is also the winter solstice, a date of profound importance to many cultures. Galgano's story may have been manufactured specifically to replace such a feast at the Montesiepi site. Notably, they all relate to stories in the stars.

All three of the earliest texts profoundly disagree about why Galgano would go to Rome against St Michael's express instructions. The Pope was not in Rome at the time of Galgano's visit,[57] so he could not have met with him, as one text claims. Nor was any permission needed to found a monastic order until after the Fourth Lateran Council of 1215,[58] so this is a later interpolation. The remaining explanation of Galgano's excursion – to see the basilica of the Apostles since those twelve figures appeared in his vision – cannot be confirmed, although it does serve to underline the importance of the Twelve Apostles in Galgano's dream. The whole Roman visit sequence appears to be a device so that the episode with the three vandals can take place, and the idea of sending Galgano on a pilgrimage to Rome may well have been inspired by tales of St Francis.[59]

If the Cistercians manufactured the Galgano legend, then the Arthurian tale would have inspired the Galgano story, rather than the reverse.[60] The Cistercians are known for having produced the Galahad legends of the Arthurian tradition, so they certainly knew the Arthurian material. But if the Cistercians did put the Sword in the Stone, then why is the Galgano story not a closer match for the Arthurian tale? Besides, the authors of the earliest variants of Galgano's legend were not Cistercian. It makes more sense to assume that the sword was already in the stone atop Montesiepi – and under the control of a community of hermits – when the Cistercians took over the site.

The round chapel, which the Cistercians falsely claimed credit for building, was certainly already there. Once the Cistercians took over the chapel and turned it into a pilgrimage site, the same sword would have remained in place. Before that, though, there could have been many swords. The chapel may have been built around the site of a very ancient sword ritual. A pre-existing tradition of sticking swords into a stone on the site might explain why the Cistercians were unable to manufacture a tale that more closely matched the Arthurian variant, especially if the local population had strong religious associations with their own variant.

This would have been a powerful conservative force against any changes to the tradition. The presence of the Archangel Michael in the story, as well as in local traditions in many villages all over the region, suggests that we are probably dealing with a tale about a ritual that originally belonged to a sword god.[61] For instance, in some variants, Galgano is conceived through the intervention of St Michael, rather like Gabriel announcing the birth of Christ, and he is told to build a round building where he meets the Apostles instead of at the site where he plunged the Sword into the Stone. There is also a part of the cult of St Michael in which a dying knight's sword was plunged into the ground near his bed, something that is reminiscent of the sword belonging to the dead knight in the stories of Lancelot. So, what we are looking at in the Galgano legend, underneath all the material that has collected around it, is probably a restructured myth of a sword god, most likely that of the Hittites discussed in chapter 1.

The Tradition

The story of St Galgano, then, is a twelfth-century recreation of the ritual described by Herodotus on a site reputed to be a centre of worship for the Etruscans. We have a *kurgan*-like hill with a stone-pit grave, topped with an embedded sword, the hilt of which matches one type of steppe nomad blade, although carbon dating puts it at 1100–1300 CE. We have severed hands at the site. We have St Michael, who can be shown to have supplanted several war gods in Christianised stories. We have a box with wood in it instead of bones. We have a hermit at the site of a grave, and if the body in the grave is not Galgano's, whose body is it, and when was it put there? Was he keeping watch over the site of the grave? The parts of the story that do not match the ritual (the wild early years, the living in a cave before moving to the hermitage, living with animals, etc.) can be traced to another saint, William of Malavalle (who happened to be French), in a nearby valley; they are probably not original to the Galgano legend.

Galgano came from an illiterate family, so their local lore was probably transmitted orally. He was blond, so there is a chance his family's presence in Italy traces to the Norman settlement there during the Crusades. If the family is Norman, that could be another link to how they knew the ancient ritual with the sword, which we will discuss in chapter 5. If the family did not come from Normandy, that blond hair could hint at Alanic roots from another source, but there are no Alano-Sarmatian settlements anywhere near the site.

Most accounts say the Cistercians built the chapel, but it actually looks as if they did not acquire it until after it was built, since construction took place between 1181 and 1185. The Cistercians had huge libraries and were largely responsible for transmitting the Alano-Sarmatian elements of the Arthurian tradition, and although they do not seem to come into the picture until after this ball was already rolling, this could indicate that the ritual was still remembered on a rather wide basis even in the twelfth century.

All things considered, we arrive at the inescapable conclusion that someone alive in 1181 knew of a 1,500-year-old ritual that had once taken place in the hills near Siena and adapted it to a Christian setting, thus transmitting the motif of the Sword in the Stone and forming a connection with the Arthurian legends that is still widely acknowledged to this day.

PART II

THE SWORD IN
THE ALTAR

5

THE SCYTHIANS AND THE SWORD
IN THE ALTAR

The first evidence of a sword embedded in wood comes from Herodotus, who recorded it in the fourth century BCE.[1] Each Scythian capital had a temple dedicated to 'Ares'. We know that wasn't the name of the Scythian sword god any more than 'Ares' was the name of the Alan sword god. These are the names the Greeks and the Romans gave to other people's gods when they did not know what the indigenous worshippers called their deities. This steppe god, though, is one of the most vicious war deities ever to charge out of myth and onto the altars of men. It turns out that the Roman Mars is more complicated than the other gods of the pantheon. His mother was Juno, the Hera of the Roman pantheon. But his father wasn't Jupiter. It was a red rose given to Juno by the Roman goddess Flora. We are not even precisely sure that Flora was a Roman goddess. She is more than a little intermingled with a goddess who seems to have been worshipped on the Eurasian steppes.

The confusion goes on. Mars is also a god of agriculture, possibly because the planet dominates the sky during March, near the beginning of spring when the constellation Aries is the main feature in the sky – the same Aries we met with Jason and the Golden Fleece. This is the time for planting, which seems to be an odd thing for a nomadic tribe to celebrate since the main feature of their lives is that they moved around and did not settle down long enough to grow anything. Maybe this is one of those cases where the Roman deity is not an exact match for the foreign deity. Or maybe the connection with the goddess overruled that.

Mars was also said to come from Thrace, which was an approximate starting point for the Alan invasion of the Roman Empire. Perhaps that was part of the connection. Also, the oldest version of Mars that the Romans knew had a unique sacrifice: he was the only Roman god to whom horses were sacrificed. Perhaps that had something to do with the burial practices of horse-riding nomads, who included, among other things, horses, sometimes just the head (which seems to be the focus of the Roman sacrifice) in their graves. The Roman ceremony for this celebration was called Equus October, the October Horse. The festival marked the end of military campaigning and the beginning of the harvest season. The two most prominent animals sacrificed to Mars, though, were the ram and the bull, as seen in other stories we have looked at from the Hittites to the Greeks. Once again, we have a reference to what is happening in the sky, with both creatures remembered in the constellations of Aries and Taurus.

In Book IV of his *History*, Herodotus described the ceremony honouring the sword god in Scythian cities as taking place on a large 'hill'. He wrote that an ancient iron sword was embedded in wood atop the temple. Herodotus went on to note that 150 'wagon loads' of brush were hauled in and piled on top of the temples once a year. This was because the wood pile would shrink as a result of rain and natural decomposition, leaving a layer of soil covering these temples. Herodotus' description adds more details.

> In every district, at the seat of government, Ares has his temple; it is of a peculiar kind, and consists of an immense heap of brushwood, three furlongs each way and somewhat less in height. On top the heap is levelled off square, like a platform, accessible on one side but rising sheer on the other three... Annual sacrifices of horses and other cattle are made to this sword, which, indeed, claims a greater number of victims than any other of their gods. Prisoners of war are also sacrificed to Ares, but in their case the ceremony is different from that which is used in the sacrifice of the animals: one man is chosen out of every hundred; wine is poured on his head, and his throat cut over a bowl; the bowl is then carried to the platform on top of the wood-pile and the blood in it poured out over the sword. While this goes on above, another ceremony is being enacted below, close against the pile; this consists of cutting off the right hands and arms of the prisoners who have been slaughtered and tossing them into the air. This done, and the rest of the ceremony over, the worshippers go away. The victims' arms and hands are left to lie where they fall, separate from the trunks.[2]

The type of structure being described is a *kurgan*, a burial complex used by many of the nomadic steppe cultures, particularly the Scythians. *Kurgans* first appeared in the Late Neolithic Period and were used by nomads through the mid-to-late first millennium CE.[3] Layers of earth alternated with vegetation beneath the bodies in the Bronze and Early Iron Age.[4] According to Evgenij Cernenko, 'Herodotus' story was confirmed by the archaeological excavations near Zaporozhye.'[5] Piles of sand had replaced the brushwood, giving us a clear transition from the earlier Sword in the Wood to the Sword in the Ground in this culture. The pile at Zaporozhye was 'surrounded by gravemounds dating back to the fourth century BCE. The altar itself was at least a hundred years older, since the sword found at its top dates from the fifth century BCE.'[6] The notion that the sword was supposed to be associated with wood was emphasised by the images of trees used to decorate it.[7] The connection of the sword with a graveyard was also clear. A ceremonial sword, complete with scabbard and hilt sheathed in gold, had been 'inserted ... point downwards, the pommel being barely visible above the floor-level'.[8] So here we have a connection between the stories of the sword in the ground and the sword in the tree.

Tadeusz Sulimirski, one of the leading experts in Sarmatian culture, drawing on Herodotus, thought that this type of sword worship was part of the religions of all of the Iranian-speaking steppe peoples, including the Alano-Sarmatians.[9] For instance, the explorer Mark Sykes (1879–1919) notes: 'The organisation of the Sassun tribes in the area is peculiar. They are divided firstly into the Bosikan and Kurian, who, by their own account, worshipped a sword thrust into the ground before the revelation of Mohammed.' [10] The last Iranian people to still practise the rite of venerating a sword stuck into the ground – or who at least did so at the beginning of the last century – are some of the Dimili tribes of East Anatolia, most interestingly, among them, the Sarmi.[11] He adds: 'Some Dimili Alevis, as well as the Yezidi clans, still maintain the ancient Iranis rite of worshipping the deity represented by a sword stuck into the ground.' He mentions this practice among a few Dimili tribes: essentially the Bosikan, Kurian and apparently also the Zekiri, Musi and Sarmi. But he adds that at the time the last three no longer practised it.

Sykes, in an extraordinary account of a journey though ten of the Asiatic provinces of Turkey in 1904, recorded a burial rite among the nomadic Kurds, in which they 'put a stick at either end and cover the grave with brushwood'. Could this be a remnant of the enormous pile of brushwood, possibly centred on a *kurgan*, that Herodotus described as being 'stabbed' by a sword in the Scythian tradition?

Herodotus went so far as to say that the Scythians of the North Pontic region worshipped an iron sword, or 'scimitar', as their sword god. To this day their descendants, the Circassians, include the embedding of a sword in the ground as part of their war dances.

Later, the Roman historian Ammianus Marcellinus (2.18) wrote:

> No temple or shrine is to be found among [the Alans], not so much as a hut thatched with straw, but their savage custom is to stick a naked sword in the earth and worship it as the god of war, the presiding deity of the regions over which they range.[12]

Because the Ossetians preserved the Alanic names of the characters, we know the story dates back at least to the time of the Alans. When Ammianus Marcellinus recorded the fourth-century CE Alan ritual honouring their sword god, all that was left was the ground and the sword being thrust into it,[13] backing up to the related ritual that Herodotus recorded among the Scythians in the fifth century BCE.[14]

Ares and Hephaistos are brothers, both sons of Zeus and Hera.[15] Ares probably came from Thrace, while Hephaistos from Lemnos in the Aegean, the latter possibly from a pre-Greek substratum, not unlike Athene and Okeanos.[16] The Ares out of Thrace is the same steppe sword god that Herodotus identified as the Scythian Ares. There are layers upon layers of myths in Greece with the steppe Ares and his sword tale coming out on top.

It is possible that the altar where the Scythians worshipped Ares was something not unlike the altar in the Perilous Chapel, with the dead knight beside or even beneath it (see chapter 3). The sword transferred from the wood to the ground would have the altar replaced by stone, matching even more closely to this later story.

As the Roman Empire was invaded by barbarians in the fourth century CE, the Alans came in on the wave before the Huns. These nomads from the Eurasian steppes were related to the Scythians and the lesser-known Sarmatians, leading scholars to call them either the Alano-Sarmatians or the Sarmato-Alans, depending on whether the text is being written in western or eastern Europe. Like the Sarmatians, the Alans dressed in conical hats and embroidered tunics over leather trousers and boots. They resembled in many ways a combination of the cowboys and Native Americans of the Old West, even carrying bows – though these were in the recurved style of the steppes – and lassos. The lassos in particular annoyed the Romans because the Alans were able to snag the end man on the straight Roman lines of legionaries and pull, playing a game of living dominos. As we saw, Ammianus

Marcellinus tells us they lived in wagons that carried their belongings and were driven by their women. Their children drove herds of cattle, sheep and horses. The Romans reported that they killed any man who became too old or disabled to fight in battle, which leads one to wonder what the Alans thought was 'old' in terms of years.[17]

In war, the heavily armoured Alans wore conical helms – essentially metal versions of their hats – shirts and trousers of linked armour, and leather boots, sometimes covered with links as well. The wealthier the warrior, the more elaborate the armour. They each carried a shield marked with their *tamga*, a personal symbol not unlike the heraldic symbols borne by medieval knights. They tended to fight with long cavalry swords for close combat and bows for ranged warfare. Their favourite tactic was known as the feigned retreat. Three units would line up against the opponent and charge. The centre would turn and flee at the last moment, drawing the enemy into the middle. The sides would then close on the opponent, defeating all or most of the opposing warriors. This manoeuvre stopped the advance of Atilla the Hun at Châlons in Gaul and centuries later won the Battle of Hastings for William the Conqueror in Britain.

As far back as the first century CE the Romans considered the steppe weapons to be better than their own swords.[18] This supports the idea that the steppe nomads had their own blacksmiths rather than relying on Greek and Roman smiths. The stories of the Kalybes, the famed smith tribe near the Caucasus Mountains and the Black Sea whom we discussed in chapter 1, confirm this hypothesis.

Herodotus described the ceremony honouring the sword god in Scythian cities, looking at the world through Greek eyes, while Ammianus Marcellinus observed the Alans through Roman eyes. We have no indigenous record because the Sarmatians and Alans had no written language. What we do not know, for instance, is when Ammianus Marcellinus says the Alans plunged swords into the ground whether that ground was a grave and if the sword belonged to that warrior and if it was a sword made specifically to represent the god of war or was just an ordinary sword. We do not know if there was one sword or many. What we do know is that the Romans did not have a name for the deity any more than Herodotus did and that Ammianus gave up and simply identified him as a 'god of war'. Perhaps the name was taboo. We have seen this before, with the Hittite sword god who had a stationary temple of stone just as the Scythians had one of wood. Maybe the Alans had adapted the ritual of the sword in the ground instead of into a wooden altar due to their mobile lifestyle.

Beowulf's Magical Sword

This late-Roman story of a Sword in the Ground next became the Sword in the Rocky Cave in the medieval tale of Beowulf. The basic outlines of the story can be summarised briefly as follows: Beowulf, a young nephew of Hygelac, king of the Geats, hears that the court of the Danish king Hrothgar is being terrorised by a monster named Grendel. Eager for adventure, he sails with a band of warriors across the straits that separate his homeland in what is now southern Sweden from Denmark and makes his way to Heorot, Hrothgar's mead hall. That evening, while the company sleeps, Grendel attacks, but this time he comes face to face with Beowulf. They struggle at close quarters, and, recalling the Scythian habit of severing arms, the Geatish hero tears off Grendel's shoulder with his bare hands. Mortally wounded, the monster slinks away, and the next evening, thinking all is well, Hrothgar throws a feast in honour of his guest's victory.

But all is not well. After Hrothgar and the others retire for the night, Grendel's unnamed mother attacks Heorot, seeking vengeance for her dying son. She captures one of the courtiers and drags him back to the lair she shares with Grendel, which is located in a grotto beneath a lake some distance from the hall out in the fens.

The next morning, Beowulf, who was not present in the hall at the time Grendel's mother struck, volunteers to follow her to her lair and finish the job. He and his warband set out toward the fens. Before they leave Heorot, Unferth, one of Hrothgar's thanes, gives the Geatish hero a sword named Hrunting, the first of *two* fabulous swords that will figure in the story. When they reach the lake, Beowulf leaves his band on the shore, dives in, and surfaces in the monsters' lair, which is described as a cave-like 'hostile hall'. He attacks Grendel's mother with Hrunting, but the otherwise infallible weapon proves to be useless. The ferocious she-monster throws him to the ground and is about to deliver a death blow when, in the nick of time, Beowulf spots another wondrous sword – a sword that only a hero of his prowess can successfully wield – in a pile of armour stacked against the cave wall. With it, he dispatches Grendel's mother, beheads her dying (or already dead) son, and returns to the surface in triumph, bearing the trophy.

The hardy band returns to Heorot, and this time they and Hrothgar party with no lingering fear of being devoured. Shortly thereafter, Beowulf returns to Geatland and eventually succeeds Hygelac as king.

Here again we have the sword hero descending to the Underworld or entering a graveyard to slay a monster and/or its mother, one or both of whom are threatening the survival of the hero's community.

Despite the absence of a 'Female Sword Bestower', Beowulf's two successive magical swords are similar to those wielded by Arthur and Lancelot. In the Beowulf story, after the battle the blade of the second sword wastes away from the 'heat' of the she-monster's blood, and all that is left is its hilt. This brings to mind the swords plunged into solid objects with only their hilts left. The key elements in the Beowulf story are obviously far older than the presence of Christianity in southern Scandinavia and Britain.

The Anvil in the Ground

The anvil in the ground appears in the Nart Sagas from the Caucasus Mountains. W. S. Allen first reported the story among the Abaza and John Colarusso included it as Saga 50 in his *Nart Sagas from the Caucasus*.[19] In the Abaza variant, the Divine Smith, Tlepshw, kept his anvil seven layers deep in the earth. His apprentice was Sosruquo, the two-year-old son of Satanya, the Mother of the Narts, who dressed in white and was usually found near rivers.

Sosruquo was supposed to work the bellows, but he accidentally set the forge on fire because he was so strong. He tried to make up for this by pulling Tlepshw's anvil out of the seven layers of earth, leaving it on the doorstep every morning, then putting it away at night. Tlepshw had no idea who was performing the miracle.

One day, three young men brought a scythe to Tlepshw to have him forge it into a sword because they were fighting over it.[20] The brothers were mowers, and the scythe belonged to the youngest brother, which recalls the Scythian story of the sacred golden objects (plough and yoke, battle-axe and drinking cup) falling out of the sky and being inherited by the youngest brother. Because the youngest brother had the scythe, he was always beating his older brothers at how fast they could mow. So the brothers decided to ask Tlepshw to make the scythe into a sword to stop their endless fighting.

This may seem to us a curiously unhelpful idea. Tlepshw seems to have thought the same as he said he could do the task but warned the brothers that they would fight over the sword even more than they fought over the scythe. He even offered to make a sword for each of the brothers in exchange for the scythe. The brothers refused, so Tlepshw declared that he would turn the scythe into a sword for whichever brother could lift his anvil. Each brother would have three tries.

Sosruquo stood by and watched as the brothers tried. The older two failed. The youngest brother moved the anvil but could not lift it. Tlepshw therefore kept the scythe and agreed to make the swords within three days. While the bargain was being struck, Sosruquo begged to be allowed to put the anvil away. The smith, thinking this miracle was impossible, agreed, hoping to keep the child busy while he finished his business with the three brothers. Sosruquo quickly picked up the anvil, shoved it down its usual seven layers, then pushed it down another layer to prove his point, making eight levels. (In Saga 55, which tells this story, the number is the familiar sacred number nine.)

The council of the Narts assembled and consulted a witch, who got Satanya, the Mother of the Narts, to reveal that Sosruquo was born from a rock beside a river. With that, they all decided that Sosruquo would become a mighty warrior, and presumably his sword would be made from the scythe. The fact that the hero was born from a stone seems to add another reference to the Sword in the Stone myth. That Satanya was involved brings in the 'Female Sword Bestower' tale.

The story of Sosruquo was also known to the Ossetians, who called the smith by the Alanic name Kurdalægon, and the name for Sosruquo in Ossetia, where the last speakers of an Alanic dialect live, was Soslan, which means 'breath of the Alans'.[21] In a saga found among the Ubykhs,[22] the Divine Smith helps Satanya place her infant son inside a hollowed-out stone, similar to the hollow in which Jason found his sword and the crevice into which Galgano plunged his blade. The smith 'frees' the infant from the rock, tempering him in water as one would temper a sword. This is the recurring motif of the metal man. Later, the hero is described as being driven into the ground by a sword,[23] not completely unlike what we find in the Hittite variant, as well as those of the Ogun at which we shall look in chapter 6.

In the Abazan version, 'Saga 55: How Sosruquo brought *sana* to the Narts,'[24] we find a variant of the Prometheus myth.[25] There are, however, elements of the Sword in the Stone story present. Tlepshw argued that the *sana*, the sacred drink of the Narts (rather like beer), should be given to Sosruquo to drink since he lifted the anvil out of seven layers of earth and thrust it back nine. Sosruquo drank the *sana*, using the golden cup of the *Alagaeta* (the Alan people). At the close of the saga, Satanya placed an *Abra* stone from a meteorite (an iron-nickel alloy), the heaviest type known, on the lid of the *sana* barrel.

In a variant from the Ubykhs that is similar to the Theseus variant, Satanya appears as the mother of Yarichkhaw, who hides weapons left behind by her son's father underground.[26] When the hero is twenty years old he reaches manhood, securing his father's horse, sword and lance from underground.[27] The implication is that the father is dead and that the horse, sword and lance are in his grave. In this case, the hero saddles the horse while his mother fetches the weapons. Later, the hero plants the lance in the ground, a detail that shows up in Irish myths (see chapter 7), and seven brothers fail to pull it out. Yarichkhaw pulls the lance free with ease. He then sits on a chair, which sinks seven layers into the earth. The story concludes that when Yarichkhaw's horse sinks beneath the ground, the end of the world will be at hand.[28]

Here we have the story of the anvil thrust into the earth, much as the sword – or the sword and anvil – feature in the Arthurian episode. The Alans of the fifth century CE appear to have carried the story to Gaul, in particular Burgundy, where many of them settled and where Robert de Boron later picked up the detail that the sword was connected with an anvil as well as with a stone. The fact that the *Abra* stone is part of a meteorite once again brings in the starry resonance.

A very different aspect to this ever-shifting, ever-spreading motif comes from West Africa, and adds yet more layers to this complex story.

6

THE WEST AFRICAN SWORD IN THE EARTH

The stories we have examined so far occur in the Northern Hemisphere. We will now look at an outlier, which came to the West via the slave trade with the Americas – specifically from Yorubaland. Though there are many proffered translations, Richard F. Burton, in 1863, seems to have hit closest to the mark by deriving the Yoruba term 'Ori Obba', or 'Head King'.[1] This may be a reference to the political system, which resembled that of the Alano-Sarmatians, where the people elected a Head King when they needed someone to negotiate or command them as a group. Other than that, the social organisation was fairly loose. In 1985 Thomas Lawson observed that there is a scholarly debate about 'whether the establishment of the Yoruba people as a distinct tradition is traceable to migrations of people from the Middle East or whether they are the result of a culture born of contact between indigenous African forest people and people from the dry regions beyond the Niger River'.[2] Although it was beyond the scope of Lawson's research, there are striking parallels between the worship of Ogun, the West African god of the hunt, iron and war, and the sword god of the ancient Scythian and related steppe cultures, who were responsible for the transmission of the sword story to the Middle East.

Like Mithras, Ogun was a god of contracts, and oaths were sworn to him on iron. He is known as both a blacksmith and a warrior. We find the same ideas associated with the Scythian sword god and his heroic reflexes in later tales, such as that of the Sword in the Stone from the Arthurian tradition.[3] Here we will consider parallels and the extent to which the Yoruba and the attendant Dahomean beliefs surrounding Ogun were influenced by ancient Scythian religious beliefs, some possible routes by which these beliefs spread to West Africa, and when this might have happened.

Ogun served as the 'the god of hunting, iron and warfare' in much of West Africa.[4] From there slaves carried his worship to the Caribbean, South America and North America (c. 1500–1865 CE).[5] In Yorubaland, he was the god of metals and creativity,[6] associated with both the destructive and constructive use of tools, including weapons. According to Lawson, 'Ogun's status reflects duality. His abode is both in the heavens and on (or under) the earth. He is therefore both a living god and a dead ancestor.'[7] We saw this same duality with the Hittite sword god. The Dahomean variant is more explicit. There Ogun's story has the deity brought to earth by the Creator in the form of a sword. The Creator used the sword 'to clear the forest and taught people to build houses and till the soil ... [and] how to use metal'.[8] This is an explicit reference to the story transmitting along with the knowledge of how to forge iron.

As the story goes, Ogun was the first king of Ife. When some of his followers were disrespectful, he killed them with his sword. Eventually he killed himself with his own sword, but his followers say that at Ire-Ekiti – a township situated in Ekiti State, south-west Nigeria, that was supposedly founded by Ogun – he disappeared into the Earth. One Yoruba story tells how Ogun sank into the earth while holding onto a long chain, not unlike the one Zeus hung on. He told his people that he would come to their aid in their time of need if they pulled on the chain.[9] A townsman pulled on the chain to test Ogun, and he sprang out of the earth, decapitating the man when he realised he had been tricked. In another variant, 'Ogun inadvertently killed his own townspeople and ... committed suicide by falling on his sword.'[10]

In general, after Ogun slaughtered several of his own people because they were not respectful toward him, 'he killed himself with his own sword and disappeared into the bosom of the earth. His last words were a promise to respond to those who called upon him in dire need.'[11] This brings to mind Arthur sleeping under a mountain. In medieval tradition, Arthur lies either beneath Mount Etna in Sicily or somewhere in Britain. Throughout Britain there are a number of sites, notably the Eildon Hills and Alderley Edge, where Arthur is believed to be sleeping until recalled by his people. A similar story is told about Charlemagne, whose people also had contact with the steppe riders, while Theseus, whom we saw as having a strong role in the sword motif, is believed to sleep beneath the Acropolis in Athens. Another Yoruba variant in which Ogun is the god of thunder, and hangs himself after inadvertently killing his wives and children, echoes tales of Hercules. We also find strong parallels to the Nart Sagas, where Batraz kills over half of his followers and then essentially commits suicide by ordering his followers to dispose of his sword following his death (also consider Arthur's commanding Griflet or Bedivere to throw Excalibur into a lake or the sea before he is carried away to Avalon at the end of his earthly existence).

The parallels go far beyond the surface of the traditions. Ogun is a warrior god, represented by a sword/sabre being driven into the ground in front of an altar.[12] This is remarkably similar to Herodotus' well-known account of the Scythian rituals to their war god.[13] There is also an explicit connection between blacksmiths and the kingship, as evidenced by a shrine to the 'first mythical blacksmith', which is located 'within the palace walls and used by chiefs for debating judicial matters and swearing oaths'.[14] The foregoing can be compared to the major role played by the Divine Smith Kurdalægon, minus the juridical aspect, in the Nart Sagas, in which he forges the Nart leader Batraz's magical sword. In Norse, Germanic and British traditions, which we will explore next, the Divine Smith Weyland forged magical swords for the sword heroes Beowulf and Seigfried.

In the Indo-European traditions, as described by the late Georges Dumézil, sovereign or 'first function' deities tend to be associated with the colour white; 'second function' or warrior deities are associated with red, and 'third function' or fertility gods and goddesses are associated with blue or green.[15] In Dahomey (located in modern Benin), the colours associated with the worship of the gods are identical: white, red and blue. The red stands for Ogun, and red clothing is frequently featured in ceremonies that honour him.[16] There is also a tripartite division with respect to Ogun among those who use iron. Blacksmiths, woodcarvers and body artists form one group; hunters, warriors and people who tap trees (for sap) form a second; farmers form the third.[17] This corresponds rather neatly to a tripartite division, which is characteristic of Indo-European rather than West African traditions. Sacrifices offered to the first two groups are 'blood' (from humans or from wood) and dog blood (particularly with the blood poured on a stone), with the ritual emphasis on 'the proper 'feeding' of iron'.[18]

Like the steppe war god, Ogun was associated with thunder and lightning as well as with a woman connected to water.[19] The 'Amazons' lent their name to the female warriors of the Dahomean king, who swore by 'thunder and lightning'.[20] The steppe nomads most closely connected to the 'Amazons' were the Sarmatians, or 'Sauro-Sarmatians', whose sword god presided over thunder and lightning.[21] Just as Arthur has his Lady of the Lake, a water deity, the river goddess Osun, another 'Female Sword Bestower', is associated with Ogun.[22] In the stories from the steppes the water women and the sword god are also linked with death. We find this same detail in a Haitian story where Ogu-Badagri, the master of lighting and storms, warned a woman in a dream that her visitors were the dead.[23]

Ogun is known as 'the possessor of two machetes: with one he prepares the farm, and with the other he clears the road'.[24] This description calls to mind the traditions of Arthur, Lancelot and Beowulf having two swords. With Arthur, the connection is extremely explicit in the Middle English poem called the Alliterative *Morte Arthure*, in which his blades are Clarent and Claris, War and Peace.[25] The original Sword from the Stone, which broke in Arthur's fight with King Pellinore at the beginning of his reign, was actually just his first sword; Excalibur, given to him by the Lady of the Lake, was his second. There is nothing, however, to indicate that such details came to West Africa through the Arthurian tradition being spread by European colonisation and the Church; the rest of the Matter of Britain is completely missing. This suggests that the elements that survive here come from a source that was common to both traditions, and we believe that source to be the steppe sword god. As Sulimirski points out, the 'worshipping of the iron sword' and the Mars-like god associated with it was deeply embedded in the religion of the ancient Sarmatians and Alans from the earliest period in their history,[26] and they spread the story to others. In Yorubaland we literally have a sword god plunging into the Earth, like the Hittite sword god, combined with a story that reflects Arthur's tale that he will return to save his people in their time of need.

As C. W. von Sydow long ago pointed out, tales don't move, people do,[27] and what we may have here is transmission by nomads. Since the technological process for forging iron seems to have been transmitted in conjunction with the tales, a route through the kingdom of Meroe, in what is now eastern Sudan, becomes possible. This does not mean that the Kushites, who ruled Meroe, themselves needed to be the ones carrying the knowledge. There may have been a route through Meroe that someone transferring the tales of the Scythian/Alano-Sarmatian sword god could have used.

The Head King traced his power back to Oduduwa, a foundational ancestor of the people. 'The people' are a bit hard to define as well, since those living where Yorubaland is today were not called 'Yoruba' in the seventh century BCE. More importantly, Eurasian DNA has been found in Yoruba samples, and some scholars speculate that it was introduced during the period when the Sahara was covered with lakes and vegetation some 7,500–10,500 years ago.[28] But perhaps the transmission was more recent. After all, the window of active ironworking from this site is *c.* 300 BCE to *c.* 200 CE.[29] The use of tiny iron implements as symbols of Ogun date back at least 500 years.[30] Babalola suggests an even earlier date, pointing to Ogun's presence in songs and legends associated with hunting.[31] The date of collection may account for the time difference here, since we are once again dealing with a people without a written language.

Maybe the Kushites were the transmitters, after all. Their sword god is a lion-headed figure, Apedemak, who, at first glance, bears no relation to Ogun. The lion-headed Apedemak does, however, call to mind the lion heads on the hilt of the Hittite sword god's weapon. The sword carried by the Kushite dancers is of a similar shape, and the god himself is plunged into the ground. This raises a question: when Ammianus Marcellinus said that the Alans worshipped the sword as a god of war, did that mean that the Alans literally saw the sword itself as a god of war? Apedemak's sacred animals, curiously, were elephants and cattle (including bulls), and one of Ogun's followers, Erinlé, appears as an elephant that disappeared into the Earth and emerged as a river.[32] That makes Apedemak almost a perfect 'bridge' figure between the Scythian/Alano-Sarmatian god and Ogun.

It is also possible that another ancient people could have used the Saharan route through the territories of the Garamantes – who were descended from Berber tribes and lived south of Libya, which was part of Numidia, a kingdom that has come up in our discussion of Mithras – to travel south instead of the knowledge being transmitted by the Garamantes themselves. The Vandals and Alans invaded North Africa in the fifth century CE and ruled, with Carthage as their capital, for roughly 100 years.[33] The Vandals and Alans then merged with the 'Romano-Berber population and became subjects of … Byzantium'.[34] As we have seen, the Alans knew the rituals of the steppe sword god, including one where they plunged a sword into the ground. So, if the story had not transmitted from the Caucasian steppes to West Africa by either of the other two routes we have previously discussed, the presence of these Alans in North Africa and their subsequent absorption into the Romano-Berber population provides a third opportunity for transmission.

The Slave Trade

An important thing to note about Yoruba religion is that it seems to come from diverse traditions rather than a common source.[35] According to oral history, the progenitor, Oduduwa, came from the east, sometimes specified as Ife, where Ogun ruled, while at other times it is simply associated with the general easterly direction.[36] This is the main direction we propose for the transmission of the tale. From this point, the story would travel further west. While the Yoruba supposedly banned the sale of their own people to the slave trade,[37] a large percentage of the slaves came from that population.[38] The Yoruba people also sold captives they enslaved from surrounding populations to whom some of their stories and traditions had spread.[39] The Yoruba people settled in present-day Ghana in the region of James Fort, which they built and which loomed large in the slave trade. Among these people, those possessed by Ogun may be referred to as 'horses', suggesting a connection with horse riders.[40] Additionally, the warrior god Ogu-ferraille, 'in the guise of St James the Elder', is represented by a rearing horse on an army flag.[41] Once again, something is clearly going on here with horses and swords.

Yoruba people begin to appear in the Americas between 1500 and 1800 CE, largely because of the Atlantic slave trade. Some slaves from Yorubaland settled in Haiti.[42] There we find a variant of the Sword in the Stone in a voodoo ceremony in which a knife is embedded in sand during a service to worship Ogun.

In Haiti, the Yoruba deities Shango and Ogun merged into a single deity, Ogou Chango,[43] but even among the Yoruba themselves there was the sense that the two figures belonged together as one.[44] For instance, when Yoruba slaves were Christianised by their owners in North America, Ogun became St Jacques Majeur (St James the Greater, the son of Zebedee). Storm master Ogu-Badagri, meanwhile, is the *loa*, or spirit, associated with Ezili, a goddess in the voodoo religion in Haiti.[45] Known elsewhere as Erinlà,[46] Ezili is also associated with water, as are so many other women who appear in the sword tradition.[47] What is interesting here is that in Yoruba Shango is connected with thunder and lightning and that Ogun is the warrior god,[48] which perfectly fits a split of attributes for the Scythian/Alano-Sarmatian sword god, who was traditionally associated with thunder and lightning. In Haiti, the two attributes got back together.

Ogun was considered to be one of the oldest *orishas* (spirits) known to the Yoruba, and his religion was widespread even among the tribes who bordered them. It is therefore no surprise that this aspect of worship came with them to the Americas, but some adjustments had to be made. For instance, a knife replaced the machete, since no owner was going to let a slave have a sword – though Ogun himself is still described as carrying an iron sword and wearing the red sash of a warrior. The ground became either sand or fertile ground, depending on where the slaves were held. Rags for clothing remained, but we have no record of the slaves using blue dye, charcoal or white powder to decorate their faces.

While in Africa the altar to Ogun tended to be outdoors, near a tree or a blacksmith's furnace, in Haiti the altar tended to be hidden from view, on the floor behind the front door of the lodging.[49] His focus was still on avenging injustice, and prayers to him were expected to elicit his help. Perhaps the prayers worked, for Yoruba slaves were among those who most commonly found their way back to Africa.

The transmission was not limited to North America. In a dance for Ogun in Bahia, Brazil, there are references to the god of the hunt, the god of herbalism, the god of disease, the goddess of deep water, the goddess of the rainbow, the goddess of water, the goddess of salt water, the goddess of fresh surface water, the goddess of wind and war, the god of thunder and lightning, and the god of creativity.[50] He is symbolised most frequently by a sword in Brazil.[51] This is exactly the same complex of deities that we find associated with the Alano-Sarmatian sword god.

Early Ironworkers

We have several times seen an important connection between the working of iron and the story of the embedded sword, as represented by the anvil set atop the stone. Sandra Barnes, an expert on the history and religions of Africa, suggests that the spread of Ogun's worship in West Africa accompanied the spread of the knowledge of ironworking, what she calls the 'sacred iron complex'.[52] Barnes argues that Ogun was generated, in part, by *bricoleurs*, although Armstrong thinks the materials for the creation of Ogun were already in West African cultures prior to the arrival of the iron-smelting process.[53] If Armstrong is right, the matrix may have been carried there by steppe warriors who carried the knowledge of forging iron with them, making Barnes right as well.

The Kalybes, the Caucasian steppe tribe from whom the name Excalibur most likely derived and whom we have encountered before, were responsible for figuring out how to work iron and steel into weapons 'towards the end of the first half of the second millennium' BCE.[54] The techniques developed by the Kalybes diffused across Eurasia,[55] but opinions are divided as to whether the Kalybes are the ultimate source for the knowledge of iron smelting in Nigeria or whether the process was discovered independently in West Africa.[56] Since intermediate forms of metalworking, such as copper and bronze, are unknown in West Africa prior to the appearance of ironworking, the growing consensus has been that the knowledge of how to work iron came from somewhere outside the local population.[57] Barnes and Ben-Amos believe that the ironworking process arrived in sub-Saharan Africa *c.* 500 BCE and spread to 'most areas of the subcontinent' by 300 CE.[58] They argue that the process could have arrived 'as early as 600' BCE.[59]

By the time the story of Ogun gets to Haiti, Ogu-balindjo is the god who protects people from drowning at sea.[60] According to Métraux, 'Ogu-balindjo ... lives right in water and must be constantly sprinkled with water whenever he leaves his element'.[61] In West African tradition, water from 'a blacksmith's forge is used to cool [a warrior/hunter] down'

The Hittite weather god Teshub.
(Courtesy of Dosseman, Creative
Commons CC-BY SA 4.0)

The Hittite sword god at Yazilikaya.
(Courtesy of Klaus-Peter Simon,
Creative Commons CC-BY SA 3.0)

Left: Statue of Herodotus in old Halicarnassus, modern Bodrum, in Turkey. (Shutterstock)

Below: Single-horn blacksmith's anvil. (Courtesy of Andrew Butko, Creative Commons CC-BY SA 3.0)

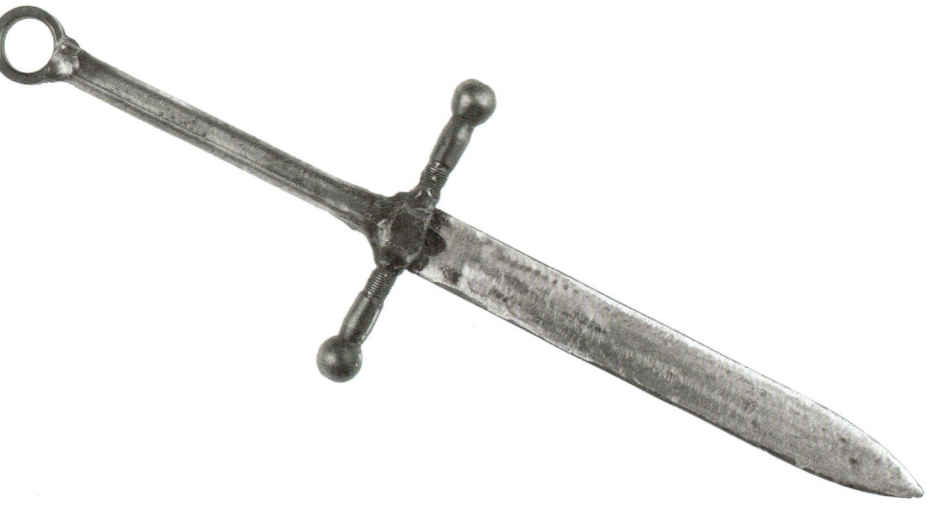

An ancient iron sword from the steppes. (Shutterstock)

A coin from *c.* 120–150 depicting Theseus discovering the sword beneath the stone. (Courtesy of the Staatliche Museen zu Berlin, Münzkabinett / Reinhard Saczewski, Public Domain 1.0)

Left: Jason with the Golden Fleece by Bertel Thorvaldsen. (Courtesy of the Thorvaldsen Museum, CC0)

Below: Theseus Finding His Father's Sword and Sandals by Jean Lemaire. (Courtesy of the Statens Museum for Kunst, CC0)

Mithras slaying the bull. Rome, second to third century BCE. (Courtesy of the Metropolitan Museum of Art)

Reconstruction of the Mithraic Temple from Dura Europos. (Courtesy of Yale University Art Gallery, CC0)

Arthur pulls the sword from the stone in an illustration by Walter Crane. (**Courtesy of the** New York Public Library, CC0)

Seventeenth-century illustration of the Temple of Diana, Londinium. (Public domain)

Above left: Galahad pulls Balin's sword from the floating stone in an illustration by Arthur Rackham. (Courtesy of the University of California Libraries, CC0)

Above right: A stained-glass window depicting St Wulfstan, in St John's Church, Bedwardine, Worcester, England. (Courtesy of Medarduss, Creative Commons CC-BY SA 4.0)

A fanciful depiction of the sword in the anvil. (Shutterstock)

Above: Galgano's Sword in the Stone today. (Courtesy of Alexmar983, Creative Commons CC-BY 4.0)

Below: San Galgano Abbey. (Adobe Stock, 168771251)

Sarmatian Akinak sword decorated with animals in Scythian-Sarmatian style. (Shutterstock)

Beowulf slays Grendel in an illustration by John Henry Frederick Bacon. (Courtesy of University of Toronto, CC0)

Above: Orisha deities depicted in Brazil. Ogun would have been one of these gods, which were first transmitted to the Caribbean from Yorubaland. (Courtesy of Turismo Bahia, Creative Commons CC-BY SA 2.0)

Left: Ogun as an embedded sword. (Shutterstock)

Below: Sigurd and Regin at the forge. Woodcarving from the Sigurd Portal of the Hylestad stave church, Norway, *c.* 1200 BCE. (Courtesy of the Norwegian Directorate for Cultural Heritage, CC0)

Fionn mac Cumhail and
the Fianna, as illustrated
by Stephen Reid. (Public
domain)

Volsung attempts to
withdraw the sword from
the tree in an illustration by
Arthur Rackham. (Public
domain)

Above: The sword in the rock at Rocamadour. (Courtesy of Patrick Clenet, Creative Commons CC-BY SA 3.0)

Below: Contemporary sculpture which shows Odin thrusting the sword into a rock. (Shutterstock)

Emperor Yamato-Takeru. (Courtesy of Naokijp, Creative Commons CC-BY SA 3.0)

Susanoo slaying Yamata no Orochi. Early modern woodblock print by Tsukioka Yoshitoshi. (Public domain)

Constellation of Aries. (Shutterstock)

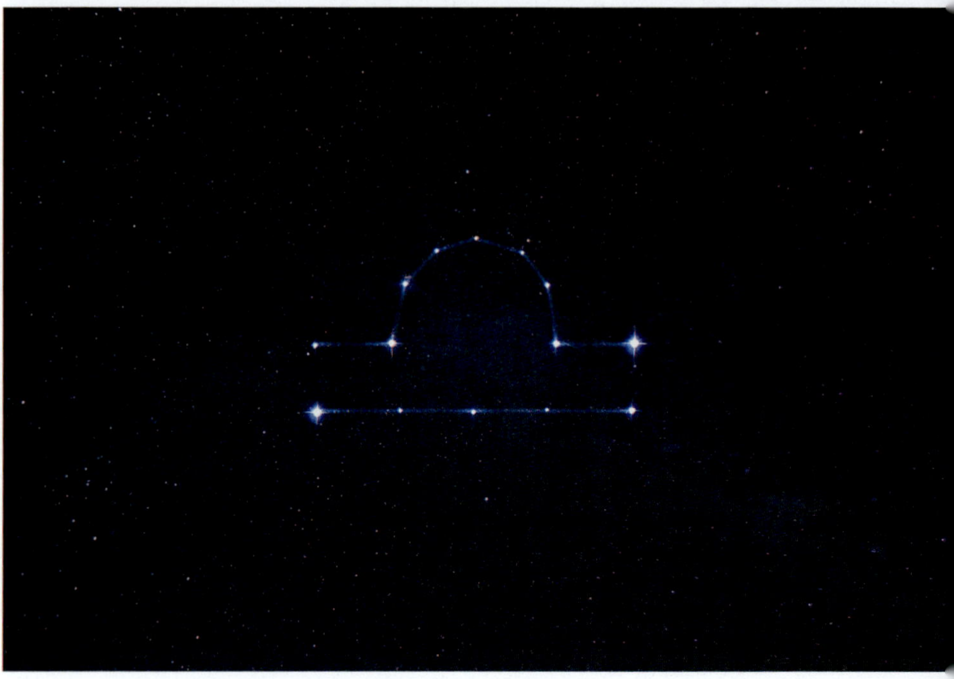

Constellation of Libra. (Shutterstock)

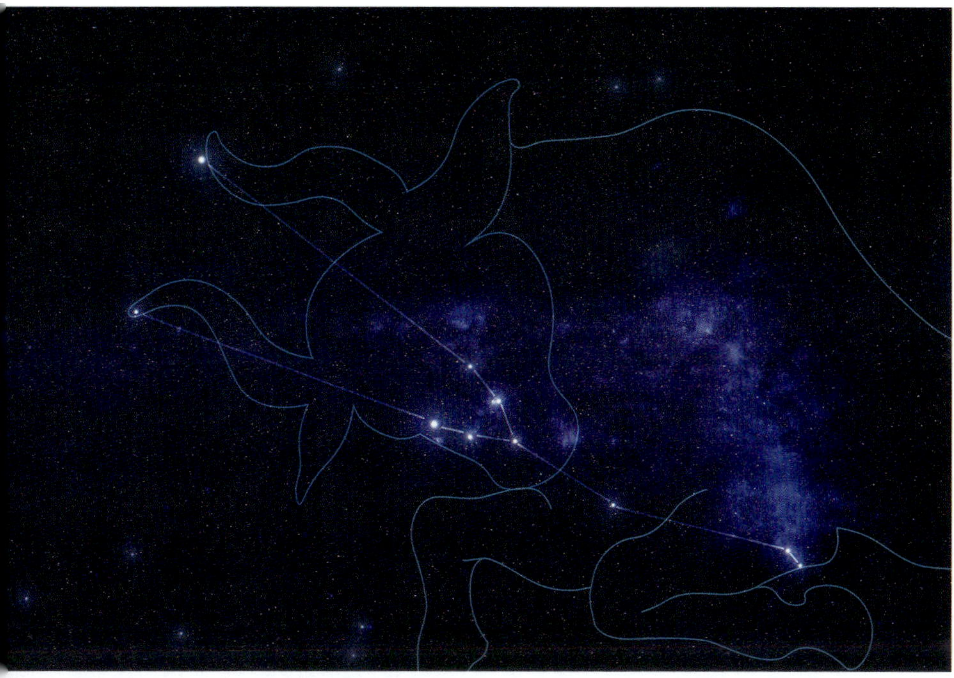

Constellation of Taurus. (Shutterstock)

The *Sverd i Fjell* (Swords in Rock) monument in Stavanger, Norway, commemorating the Battle of Hafrsfjord. (Shutterstock)

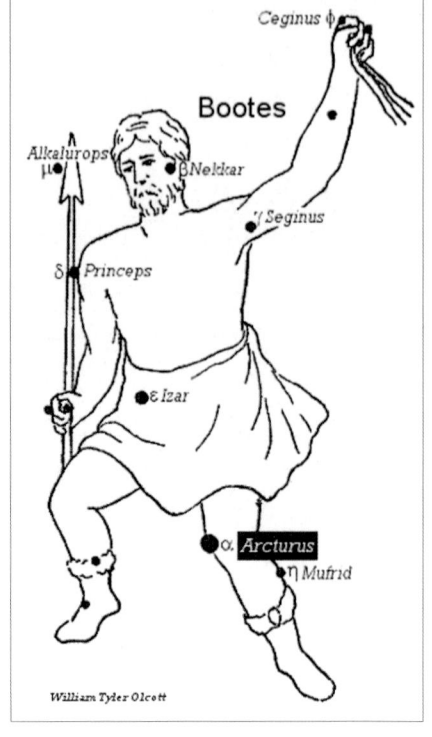

Above: Frontispiece to *The Perfect Art of Navigation* by John Dee. (Author's collection)

Right: A map of the constellation Bootes, including Arcturus, by William Tyler Olcott. (Author's collection)

after he made a kill.[62] In Irish mythology the hero Cú Chulainn has to be cooled in a similar fashion whenever he sees a group of women, while in the Nart Sagas the warrior Batraz is cooled soon after his birth by seven cauldrons of water provided by the blacksmith Kurdalægon.[63] These stories repeat among several peoples who tell of the Sword in the Stone, and it raises the possibility that the god Ogun originally came from the same source: the Eurasian steppes.

Indeed, Ogun's festival 'is said ... [to be] the oldest festival or the first festival in Ila'.[64] We suggest that the introduction of the god who became Ogun happened long before that. There is certainly evidence that indicates the cult was introduced to the region at the same time as the process of forging iron.[65] Armstrong believes some of the pieces of the tradition 'may well have roots that extend far more deeply into the past' than the date of the arrival of ironworking in the Taruga valley, but he thinks those roots are in local traditions.[66] We think those roots stretch out of Africa, all the way back to the steppe cultures of the Caucasus Mountain region.

There is an association with ironworking and the oldest references to smiths and their magical powers. It was through Egypt that the smiths in Meroe in the Republic of Sudan probably learned to work iron.[67] The hypothesis that refugees from the destruction of Meroe (*c.* 350 CE) brought the knowledge of ironworking with them to Nigeria has been rejected because of the dates of the furnaces at Taruga (*c.* 300–275 BCE), but it is possible that the knowledge could have come through Meroe at an earlier date, since Meroe shows evidence of ironworking *c.* 500 BCE.[68]

Evidence of ironworking in the Nok culture of the Taruga valley dates to the early third century BCE. Ironworking in

Nigeria at Daima near Lake Chad dates to the 'fifth or sixth century' CE.[69] Carthage, traditionally founded *c.* 800 BCE, began working with iron even earlier.[70] The North African city had heavy contact with the Garamantes, a people who drove horses hitched to chariots and who were known to live close to the Niger River.[71] This Berber-speaking people, mentioned by Herodotus, according to Shaw, picked up the knowledge of ironworking from the Carthaginians and transmitted it southward to the region that would become Nigeria.[72]

Thus, Ogun appears to be an Indo-European sword god who was himself planted in the earth. He is associated with iron – his shrine is an iron cauldron in the Hattian religion and one of his iron tools is the anvil. His story may have been transmitted along with the knowledge of ironworking by three possible routes from the Eurasian steppes. Another route from the steppes carries us into Europe when the sword is not in a stone but rather in a tree.

PART III

THE SWORD IN THE TREE

7

THE GERMANIC, ICELANDIC AND IRISH SWORDS

The Scythians were not the only people who plunged a sword into wood. The Germanic peoples also practiced this ritual, and scholars have long pointed to the Arthurian version of the Sword in the Stone and the Norse story of the 'Sword in the Branstock', a special tree, as examples of the parallel development of an Indo-European myth that became part of an epic tradition in the Celtic and Germanic cultures.[1] Instead, we suggest that they represent two variants of the same tale that diffused across Eurasia. The main reason that scholars have assumed that the Germanic variant of this legend is the product of parallel development instead of diffusion is that the Germanic sword is very clearly embedded in a tree rather than in an anvil or a stone. When the Germanic tale is viewed through its proper lens, however, it quickly becomes apparent that this difference is a matter of perspective rather than a material difference.

Tacitus' *Germania* is our main source for ethnographic data regarding the early Germanic peoples.[2] Cassius Dio, Ammianus Marcellinus and a few other Greco-Roman authors round out the very short list of written texts we have about this culture prior to their Christianisation by missionaries in the late eighth century.[3] The embedded-sword story most likely spread first to Iceland via the Viking settlement of 874 CE, and Iceland was officially Christianised by 1000 CE.[4] Snorri Sturluson, who composed the *Prose Edda*, which included the tale of the sword in the tree, in the early thirteenth century CE did not live until two centuries later (1178–1241 CE).[5] The text contains elements of the *Poetic Edda*, which was compiled before the prose version, in the late tenth century CE from even earlier sources. Germanic myths appear anywhere from that date to the High Middle Ages and are, thus, not primary sources. The Greco-Roman cultures used the sword in both the stone and the bull and show evidence that they remembered that the story was in the stars. The sword in the tree, however, seems to have forgotten this detail and may trace its roots to Scythian sources, deriving it from the contact between the Germanic peoples and the Alano-Sarmatians.

Archaeological evidence shows that Iceland was originally settled in the late eighth century by the Papar monks from Ireland. This group, who derived their name from the Latin *papa*, via Old Irish *athair* meaning 'father' or 'pope', were, according to the early Icelandic sagas, Irish monks who took up residence in parts of what is now Iceland before the country was invaded by the Vikings in the tenth century. It is important to note that the Vikings themselves were not an ethnic group as such, but rather a culture that took its elements from neighbouring peoples, in this case the Germanic Franks, who may have received the sword in the wood/altar/ground story from the Alano-Sarmatians.

The presence of these Irish monks forms a link with the sword legends of that country, in particular as laid out in the Fenian Cycle, which includes stories of the sword in the ground. The early Irish Celts indeed had a plethora of sword myths, several of which continued to be retold well into the nineteenth century.[6] Swords were said to speak – especially if those who wielded them failed to uphold the honour of the tribe to which they belonged or follow the later *Brehon Laws* that were operating from at least the sixth century and may well be much older, inherited from Indo-European practice along with aspects of the Gaelic language.[7]

One of the most notable swords is that known as the *Mac an Lúin* (Son of Lúin), which could 'cut through six feet of whatever substance was struck by it, and an inch beyond'.[8] This sword was made by a mythical smith named Lon mac Líomtha who is described as being one of the Tuatha de Danaan, the semi-mythical early people (or gods) of Ireland. He chose a remote place in Ireland to live because of the persecutions against magicians, witches and others at that time. The description of Lon given by the nineteenth-century scholar William Borlase in his magisterial work *The Dolmens of Ireland* is worth quoting in full:

> ... he lived in his cave in this mountain, unknown to all the Scoti except the few who lived in this immediate vicinity. He was a most extraordinary being, having three hands and only one leg. Two of the hands were in the usual position, and the third, with which he turned the iron of the anvil, while he hammered with the other two, grew from the middle of his breast. He never walked after the usual manner of man, as is obvious from his construction, but bounded from his pedestal by the elastic power of his waist and ham; whenever he ventured abroad, which was very seldom, he was observed flying over the valleys, and

bounding over the hills. He had lived a long time in Ireland before his art was in requisition, for before his time the Irish used no iron or steel implements, of war, but fought with sticks having stone, flint, and bronze heads.[9]

This sounds very much like a cosmogonic myth, as is the case with many of the smith gods we have encountered, and the detail concerning the earliest use of iron to forge swords is interesting, given how often this skill connects with stories of swords or other magical weapons that are drawn from or sunk into the earth.

The astronomical aspects of the story of Lon are given great weight when we learn that he possessed a remarkable cow, known as *Glas Gaibhneach*, which gave so much milk that not even the largest pail could hold it all. Lon had apparently brought this remarkable creature from Spain. It provided food for him and his seven sons and was so huge that it had to be turned about at the end of each day then back again the next morning.[10] This again suggests a cosmological nature of the story, as well as a likely transference from Spain, from where the Alans may have reached Ireland.[11] The cow may represent the sun, as in various other mythologies, or it may be a female version of Taurus.

Of the smith, his forge, and the curious cow, the same source states:

> ... in a field called Garraidh-na-Céartan is shown a cave in a rock called Céarta Loinn Mhic Liomtha, 'The Forge of Lonn son of Líomtha', and within it the cinders and dust of the forge. The smith had seven sons – one for every day of the week – who took care of this cow, each for a day in his turn. They held her by the tail and durst not turn her about, but let her go

wherever she wished to graze during the day until sunset, when they turned her face towards her bed, and then she returned home directly.[12]

At this time Lon heard of the mighty Fenian warriors and went to see their captain, Fionn Mac Cumhail. He declared that he was Lon and added, 'I am acquainted with the intricacies of every art, but my particular art is that of the smith.'[13] He then offers a contest that he will go as fast as he can back to his home, and if they can overtake him he will make them iron swords. He then leaps away at full speed, bounding across the mountains. He is pursued by Caoilté, the fastest runner among the Fenians, who catches up with him without any difficulty and, as he is about to enter the forge, strikes him with the palm of his hand on the back of his head and says, 'Smith, do not go into the cave alone.'

Thus, the Fenians won the right to have their swords made for them, and apparently Caoilté remained there working with Lon until, at the end of three days, Finn and several other of his warriors joined them 'and the smith sold them eight iron swords well-tempered and steeled'. Apparently after this Goll and Conan, the sons of Moirné, broke the smith's anvil – 'but not until they had had several swords made for themselves'.[14]

Irish traditions concerning the Sword in the Stone are few and far between. They may well have existed but, like any clear sign of a creation myth, have long since vanished. One or two small gleams do still exist – mostly concerning *The Cattle Raid of Cooley* (the *Táin Bó Cúailnge*) and the actions of the giant warrior Fergus Mac Roích.

At the heart of the saga of the *Táin* is a mighty conflict between two bulls, which, like those of the Persian god Mithras (see Chapter 8), represents a cosmic battle between two original powers. Bruce Lincoln, in his book *Priests, Warriors and Cattle* (1981), suggested that this cataclysmic struggle was an Irish echo of the primal sacrifice of the first king by his priestly brother, as we see in the story of Romulus and Remus from Rome.[15] Lincoln's reconstructed paradigm established the cosmos as the Indo-Europeans knew it and added the divine and human social order. In this same part of the story we learn that Fergus had lost his unearthly sword, stolen by his enemy Ailill during one of Fergus' many erotic encounters with Queen Maeve. Fergus swears that if he gets the sword back he will sever

> ... men's elbows from forearms, men's forearms and their fists,
> men's fists and their fingers, men's fingers and their nails, men's
> nails on the crowns of their heads, men's crowns and their
> trunks, men's trunks and their thighs, men's thighs and their
> knees, men's knees and there carves, men's calves and their feet,
> Men's feet and their toes, men's toes and their nails.[16]

This is clearly no ordinary sword, but we learn more of its extraordinary power when, having retrieved it, Fergus wields it in battle, slaying large numbers of warriors. At one moment he lifts the sword high over his head, and its blade is so long that it touches the earth behind him, calling to mind the Alan sword in the ground, just as the earlier severing of arms and hands recalls the earlier Scythian ritual. At this point Fergus' fellow warrior Cormac Con Loinges reminds him he is fighting against his own kin, to which Fergus responds by asking where he should he direct his blows. This shows the sword to be a ritual weapon which, like many other weapons of this kind, cannot be sheathed until it has drawn blood or cut though something. Cormac tells Fergus to strike three distant hills, and, turning away from the conflict, he does just that. His sword, described as 'long as a rainbow', cuts the tops off three hills. He repeats this action shortly after, and the hills he cuts are afterwards referred to as *Máela Midi* (the Cropped Ones of Meath).

It is possible that this may suggest a ritual killing involving a substitute which might also be part of a cosmogonic creation myth, and, although this may seem a detour from the various swords in stones or earth or under rocks, there is a significant connection with the sword belonging to Arthur. The name of Fergus' sword is *Caladbolg* (Hard-Notcher), which is an analogue of the earliest references to Arthur's weapon, the Welsh *Caladvwlch* (Iron Striker) as it appears in the story of 'Culhwch and Olwen' from the *Mabinogion*.

Later, as the battle reaches its bloody climax, Fergus' men offer him an oath of steadfastness, which makes it clear that we are looking at a cosmogonic myth. 'We shall do so,' they say, referring to their honourable obedience to Fergus, 'for heaven is above us and earth beneath us and the sea all around us, and unless the firmament with its showers of stars fall upon the surface of the earth, or unless the blue-bordered fish-abounding sea come over the face of the world, or unless the earth quake we shall not retreat one inch from this spot until such time as you come back to us again...'[17]

Almost exactly the same oath is attributed by Strabo to the Iberian Celts serving in the Peloponnesian War, and classical authors such as Aristotle reported the Celts only feared the sky falling on them.[18] This, along with the grounding of the supernatural sword in the earth just before the battle of the mighty bulls, suggests that here, as elsewhere in the journey of the sword, there is a powerful underpinning of cosmic myth.

Beyond this, there is little else that seems to reflect the sword motif – at least not in contemporary mode to the time of its original circulation. However, there is a curious reference in a very much later text, a book written by the noted English poet Edmund Spenser, who writes:

> I reasonably conclude that the Irish are descended from the Scythians; for that they use (even to this day) some of the same ceremonies which the Scythians anciently used. As for example, you may read in Lucian, in that sweet dialogue which is entitled *Toxaris*, or *Of Friendship*, that the common oath of the Scythians was by the sword, and by the fire; for that they accounted those two special divine powers, which should work vengeance on the perjurers. So do the Irish at this day, when they go to battle, say certain prayers or charms to their swords, making a cross therewith upon the earth and thrusting the points of their blades into the ground, thinking thereby to have the better success in fight. Also they use commonly to swear by their swords. Also the Scythians used, when they would bind any solemn vow or combination amongst them, to drink a bowl of blood together, vowing thereby to spend their last blood in that quarrel: and even so to the wild Scots, as you may read in Buchanan; and some of the Northern Irish.[19]

This forms a curious overlap between the ancient Alan and Caucasian traditions and those of seventeenth-century Ireland. The references are so exact that we can see how the older tradition remained in memory several hundred years after their point of origin. Accounts of the Scythian origins for early Irish settlers are widely attested. Although this has for some time been considered folk etymology, the story may be true for the tales if not for the people who may have travelled with the memory of a story hidden in the stars.

The reference to *Toxaris* (*Friendship*) is particularly interesting in this context.[20] It takes the form of a dialogue composed by the Syrian author Lucian. Thought to have been written around 163 CE in the Roman province of Asia, it describes a conversation between an Athenian, Mnesippus, and a Scythian friend named Toxaris who discuss at length the differences between their traditions – including the reference mentioned by Spenser who probably had it from Borlase.

The Poetic Edda

Returning to the Germanic story as recorded in chapter 3 of the *Poetic Edda*, the tale specifically concerns Sigurd.[21] It tells of the wedding of Volsung's son, Siggeir. During the celebration at an ancient oak called the Branstock, Odin (the god of war and death, among other things), recognisable by his blue cloak and one eye, shows up and plunges his sword into the tree. He makes a speech, saying that whoever can pull the sword out of the tree can claim the weapon as his own. Volsung and several other warriors attending the feast attempt the feat and fail. As with many Indo-European tales, the youngest son, in this case Sigmund, succeeds at the task, though he is the tenth born instead of the traditional third. The groom, Siggeir, tries to buy the sword from him, but Sigmund declines the offer. That causes Siggeir to make a secret vow to slaughter the Volsungs and claim the sword as his own.

Through Siggeir's villainy, all the Volsungs are sentenced to death. Siggeir takes the sword from Sigmund, and the brothers are shackled to another oak, this one in a forest, where a she-wolf kills one of them every night. When Sigmund is the last prisoner left, Signy, Siggeir's wife and Sigmund's sister, frees him. The two have an affair, and Signy bears Sigmund children, the youngest son of whom is named Sinfiolti. Furious, Siggeir captures father and son and orders that they should be buried alive. The grave has a stone roof, and Signy includes Sigmund's sword among the grave goods intended for Sinfiolti. Father and son escape when Sinfiolti plunges the sword into the stone and uses the blade to cut their iron bonds. More than a little displeased, Sigmund has Siggeir burned to death and, with the sword returned to him, becomes king.

The basic elements of the embedded weapon being a sword and of the younger brother withdrawing the blade and becoming the future king are about as close as most comparisons can be. Several key parallels are contained in the material between the withdrawal of the sword and Sigmund's ascension to the kingship. Among them are that Arthur's sword in the anvil atop a stone is in a graveyard and that Sinfiotli and Sigmund use the sword from the Branstock to cut through stone and iron as they escape from a grave.

This pattern can be seen in seemingly unrelated tales. For instance, while Thor is having a piece of whetstone removed from where it is embedded in his head, he tells of making the Morning Star out of the frozen toe of the husband of the woman who is using magic to remove the stone. The woman, Grōa, became so upset by this information that the stone 'remained embedded in Thor's skull'.[22] Here there is clearly an astral connection with a warrior and a stone associated with a sword.

In another tale, as Odin hangs on the World Tree, he is pierced by a spear.[23] The World Tree, is also known as *Mímameiðr*, 'Mīmi's tree'.[24] Sigurd's foster father, the smith Mīmir, was named for this god.[25] The foster father is called Reginn in some variants. Here we have a connection between a Divine Smith and a sword in the tree, something that clearly connects the Sword in the Stone motif with the World Tree representing the celestial pole.

As we consider all of these variants, the spread of the tale and its various developments strongly suggest that transmission occurred via the steppe nomads, many of whom were allied with Germanic peoples and lived among them for over a hundred years. As these horse-riding warriors came into contact with other cultures and transmitted their knowledge of cavalry warfare and of forging iron, they also transmitted stories about the deity who oversaw both war and smithing, a combination that occurred first among the steppe nomads.

The idea of the elite horse-riding warrior emerged in Europe in the first century, *c.* 50–1 CE.[26] Warrior graves containing spurs, horse equipment and long swords appear on both sides of the Rhine as far north as central Sweden.[27] This style of grave seems to be influenced by Sarmatian burials, as these nomads tended to substitute horse equipment and/or pieces of their animals for the full horse interments that we find in the burials of other cultures. The style of cavalry equipment also seems to have been transmitted from the Sarmatians.

Strabo thought of the Germans as Celts,[28] and Cassius Dio called Roman Germania 'Keltica', reserving 'Germania' for the area 'between the Rhine and Elbe Rivers'. For Greek writers, the Celts generally 'occupied the lands to the west [and] the Scythians to the east'.[29] From this we can see that the divisions in ancient texts were not solely made on the basis of languages spoken or perceived similarities of cultures, but rather on geographic location. Caesar places the Germans between the Celts and the Scythians, with the Danube as an arbitrary dividing line that was probably chosen more as a result of his political ambitions than of any careful ethnographic observation.[30] Arthurian scholar J. D. Bruce argued that the legend of the Sword and the Stone derived from the Greek story of Theseus and the Germanic *Volsunga Saga*. As we have seen, however, the story's pattern was more widespread than those variants and parts of it appear in Herodotus' ancient account of the religion of the Scythians.[31]

Caesar considered the 'German' cavalry to be his best mercenaries.[32] It is no accident that shortly after the German cavalry units start to appear in the Roman army (48–36 BCE),[33] Sarmatian units also start service as Roman allies. For instance, Tiberius stationed the Sarmatian Iazyges between the Danube and the Tisza as Roman allies *c.* 20 CE.[34] We know that during the Marcomannic Wars of 166/7–175 and 177–180 CE, the Iazyges were allied with the Marcomanni and the Quadi, two tribes of the Germanic Suebi,[35] and in 175 CE the Romans sent to Britain 5,500 Iazyges of the 8,000 they obtained in a truce.[36] Although the sword cult has not been recorded among Sarmatians specifically, we do know that the cult was present among their cultural cousins the Alans, who had a heavy impact on Germanic groups in the fourth and fifth centuries CE.

While the Huns had significant contact with the Germanic peoples prior to the recording of the stories in the *Volsunga Saga*, Alano-Sarmatian peoples had already had a great deal of interaction with their Germanic neighbours long before the Huns appeared on the scene. After the Huns defeated the Massagetae in 175 BCE, a tribe of Sarmatians founded a kingdom and became known as the Royal Sarmatians.[37] This group is thought by several scholars to have consisted primarily of Iazyges,[38] who may have earned their title by defeating and absorbing the Royal Scythians, who were previously settled in the area where the Romans report the Iazyges. At least one of those tribes, the Bastarrae, was still in contact with the Sarmatians by the third century BCE.[39]

By 50 CE, the bulk of the Sarmatians were located in the vicinity of the Tisza and the Danube.[40] This put them in close contact with several Germanic peoples. Tacitus writes that there were several tribes who were so intermingled that he could no longer tell which was German and which Sarmatian.[41] Some Germanic swords were marked with a line topped with a carat: 'The runic symbol ↑ (Tiwaz) which represented the name of the god Tir [Tyr]. [These] were prehistoric devices, religious or magical symbols in use from ancient times.'[42] We suggest that these symbols derived from the *tamgas* of the steppe nomads that were used by the Alano-Sarmatians. Tyr's sword was worshipped by the Franks until Christianity took over the region and Tyr was replaced by the warlike Archangel Michael.[43] Here, then, we also have a sword god associated with the sky and a sword.[44]

In one German legend, recorded by the Brothers Grimm,[45] a herdsman finds a sword that is sacred to the Scythians after a cow steps on it. He removes the sword from the ground (it doesn't seem to be embedded in any particular fashion) and gives it to the great warrior Attila the Hun, who recognises it and is thrilled to possess it. The Roman writer Priscus mentioned this and made the connection between it and the story of the shepherd who followed a trail of blood from his heifer to an ancient iron sword that was buried in the ground, which he dug up and gave to Attila, who identified it as the sword of Mars.[46] This pairs nicely with tales of the Alans plunging swords representing Mars into the ground and Scythians sacrificing cattle (including bulls) to the sword of

Mars.[47] In these tales the sword was embedded in the ground rather than in a tree or an anvil or a stone.

The pattern continues throughout the Germanic and Icelandic tales, as well as those of the Irish. In the Icelandic *Saga of Hrolf Kraki*, the short sword that Frothi drives into a wooden beam is one that he originally pulled from a stone.[48] Frothi's brother Bothvar wields a long sword which he pulled from the same stone and which he carries in a scabbard made of bark.[49] The tradition of plunging a sword into wood spilled over into other lore. The Germanic peoples had a long-held belief that sticking a knife or sword 'in the door of a Fairy dwelling, will prevent the door from being closed until the intruder ... willingly exits'.[50] Along with the tale of the sword, once again we find the transmission of the knowledge of how to forge iron.

Forging Iron

As we have seen, the knowledge of ironworking first appeared in the 'second half of the third millennium B.C. in Anatolia',[51] though it likely came to the Hittites from the Kalybes. By 1270 the knowledge had spread to Greece. The Celtic Hallstatt culture shows evidence of ironworking *c.* 1000–500 BCE. Milisauskas noted that the Scythian influence in Celtic La Tène art could have come in with iron technology (*c.* 500-300 BCE),[52] and this agrees with what we find in the patterns of transmission for the tale of the Sword in the Stone and that of the Irish smith, Lom. Knowledge of ironworking first appeared among Germanic peoples *c.* 600–300 BCE. This was not, however, the same as forging swords. The Germanic peoples did not start forging iron into longer swords intended for use by cavalry until the Late Roman Iron Age, *c.* 180–400 CE, not long before the *Volsunga Saga* developed.[53]

Wayland, one of the disabled smiths of legend (the king had him hamstrung), was famous for forging swords in the Underworld. He 'may have originated in ... Germanic countries in the stories of Völundr', another name for Wayland.[54] His tale could be Indo-European in origin or diffused from the steppes along with the story of the embedded sword. While Davidson argued that Wayland gained his gigantic size in tales from the Celts and from the Saami people of Scandinavia,[55] other smiths, such as Kurdalægon in the Nart Sagas of the Caucasus Mountains, were also exceptionally large. Once again, this detail seems to have been transmitted in conjunction with the sword stories as the steppe riders spread out from their homeland.

According to local folklore, Wayland forged Durendal and two other swords, Curtane and Almace, in the Underworld. Charlemagne is able to stick all three into a steel mound. Curtana, which is presented to Ogier the Dane, sinks to the breadth of a hand and is damaged. Almace, which is presented to Bishop Turpin, makes it to the same depth without damage. Durendal, which Charlemagne keeps until he gives it to Roland, sinks to the depth of 'half the length of a man's foot'.[56]

The Germanic peoples also carried the story of the Sword in the Stone. The story of Charlemagne's warrior Roland mimics that of Arthur in many ways. In some versions he throws the sword Durendal into a poisoned stream, instead of Arthur having his knights throw Excalibur into a lake or the sea, as he is dying. In other tales Roland throws his sword at the walls of Rocamadour, France, plunging it into stone, where it can be seen to this day.

In yet others, his horn and sword are placed beneath him after he fails to destroy the sword, and his soul is carried to

Heaven by angels just as God summons Batraz to Heaven after his indestructible sword is thrown into the sea. Just as Arthur was the last hero to die at Camlann and Batraz was the last hero to die in his war with God, Roland, along with Bishop Turpin and Gualter de Hum, was one of the last three killed at Roncevaux Pass in a battle that took place in the Pyrenees in 778 against the Basques with the Moors pursuing Charlemagne's troops from Spain.

Instead of Wayland, Divine Smith of the Germanic, Scandinavian and British peoples, it was dwarves who forged Tyrfing, the sword of Svafrlami, a grandson of Odin, and he could easily cut through both iron and steel with it just as Arthur's sword could be delved into an anvil. Sigurd's sword, Gram, could also cut through an anvil.[57] Odin plunged Gram into a giant oak tree, and as noted above, Sigmund, 'the bravest of Volsung's sons,' pulled it out.[58] Likewise Batraz, the bravest of the Narts, acquires his father's sword from the Underworld (represented by a *kurgan*-like basement in his father's house, which also contained his horse and armour).

From the above we can see that the tradition of powerful weapons such as the sword of Fergus, which touched the ground and sliced the tops off mountains, and the strange iron-working smith Lom, all relate to the same stories we have been exploring throughout this book. We can see how so many of the motifs and reflexes collected here all ultimately originate in Indo-European cultures and echo throughout even non-Indo-European lands. Something, though, made the Germanic peoples add the details about the sword being thrust into and pulled out of wood in addition to remnants of the story of the Sword in the Stone. But what changed?

PART IV

THE SWORD IN THE DRAGON'S TAIL

8

THE JAPANESE SWORD

Another Excalibur-like embedded sword plays a prominent role in the mythology of a land far removed from those we have previously examined – ancient Japan. In this instance the magical blade was discovered embedded in the tail of a dragon rather than in, under, beside or on top of a stone, tree, pile of brush or the ground. The relevant Japanese narratives are two successive (and, for the most part, wholly distinct) stories involving the same sword and are both contained in the *Kojiki*, or *Record of Ancient Matters*, compiled by Ōno Susumu (712 CE) and the slightly later *Nihonshoki*, or *Chronicles of Japan* (720 CE).[1]

The story of Susanō and Yamata no Orochi begins after Amaterasu Omikami, the sun goddess, was chosen by her father, Izanagi no Mikoto, the Japanese 'Adam', to succeed him as the divine sovereign. All went well until Amaterasu's recalcitrant brother, Susanō, the 'Raging Male', challenged her right to rule the cosmos.[2] In order to settle the controversy, they performed a grand divination in which each deity magically spat out offspring: Amaterasu from pieces of Susanō's initial sword and Susanō from his sister's *magatama*, or fertility jewel. Susanō produced more children, but Amaterasu's brood contained more males, so she was adjudged the winner by the assembled gods. Susanō, however, refused to accept defeat and 'raged with victory'. He stamped down the dykes between the divine rice paddies and eventually threw a piebald horse into the divine weaving hut, thereby killing one of Amaterasu's handmaidens. At that point, Amaterasu decided to wash her hands of her brother's antics and withdrew into Ama no Iwato, or 'The Cave of Darkness'.[3] After she was tricked into reemerging from the cave by being presented with a mirror in which she thought saw another sun goddess, her fellow deities insisted that Susanō be banished from Heaven.[4]

Susanō arrived on Earth near the headwaters of the Hi River in what is now the northern part of the island of Kyushu. After noticing a pair of chopsticks floating downstream, Susanō decided to head in the opposite direction and soon found a beautiful young maiden and her parents weeping by the side of the stream. When he inquired as to the reason for their sadness, he learned that the girl, Kushinada-hime, or 'Rice Paddy Princess', would soon become an offering to a ravenous, eight-headed, eight-tailed dragon called Yamata no Orochi, literally 'Eight-Tailed Dragon', who was terrorising the region.[5]

The god identified himself and asked the girl's parents to bring him a large tub. He filled it with sake and turned Kushinada-hime into a comb, which he inserted into his hair, telling her parents to hide. When the dragon finally appeared, its eight heads immediately began drinking the sake and the creature soon became dead drunk, at which point Susanō easily slew him. When he hacked open one of Yamato no Orochi's tails, he discovered a wondrous magical sword,[6] which he named Mura-kumo no Tsurugi, or 'Assembled Clouds Sword'. After sending the sword up to his divine sister as a peace offering,[7] Susanō restored Kushinada-hime to human form, married her, and took up residence in a palace at Suga, near the site of the Izumo-taisha shrine in Shimane Prefecture, the most sacred Shinto shrine after the grand shrine of Amaterasu at Ise in Mie Prefecture.

Like the Chinese cloud dragon, Yamata no Orochi is clearly a rain bringer, hence the original name of the sword: 'Assembled Clouds'.[8] But the Japanese dragon is also clearly an 'other', a ravenous enemy that demands a constant stream of victims (Kushinada-hime's seven sisters had already been sacrificed to the beast by the time Susanō arrived on the scene).[9] In this aspect, he shares much in common with Western (or at least Indo-European) dragons, like Python, the Theban dragon slain by Cadmus, Fafnir in the stories of Sigurd, the Hittite dragon Illyuyankas, the unnamed dragon slain by Beowulf, and the monstrous, three-headed Vedic serpent Vritra, just as his slayer shares characteristics with figures such as Apollo, the aforementioned Cadmus and Beowulf, Siegfried, the Anatolian prototype of St George, and the ancient Indic sword god Indra. Indeed, the story of Indra's slaying of the multi-headed monster presents a great many parallels to the story of Susanō and Yamato no Orochi, although Indra doesn't discover a weapon in Vritra's tail.[10]

In short, the Yamata no Orochi myth is atypical among East Asian dragon stories, and the possibility that the Indo-European elements of this dragon-slaying story diffused eastward across Eurasia seems very probable. Indeed, as we shall see, it may be possible to connect Yamata no Orochi to the constellation Draco, as well as to the more benevolent Dragon in the Chinese calendar of the twelve beasts.

Two generations later, when Amaterasu sent her grandson, Honinigi, to claim the Reed Plain on her behalf,[11] he brought with him three talismans of divine sovereignty: the Mirror, the divine *magatama* (a fertility jewel similar to the one Susanō had chewed up during the aforementioned grand divination), and, last but far from least, the sword Mura-kumo no Tsurugi.[12]

The sword was not used by Honinigi's great-grandson Jimmu Tennō in his march of conquest from the island of Kyushu along the north coast of the Inland Sea to Yamato, where he became the first emperor,[13] but several generations after Jimmu's time the wondrous sword from the dragon's tail once again played a major part in Japanese mythology, this time in the saga of Yamato-takeru,[14] Japan's greatest epic hero.

Originally named Ousu, he was the younger of twin sons born to the emperor Keikō. He proved his warlike prowess early on when, in a fit of rage, he slew his older brother Ōusu. Fearing for both his life and his throne, Ousu's father dispatched him first to Izumo and then to Kumaso to put down rebellions, hoping that his recalcitrant son would not come back alive. But, like Theseus, the young prince was victorious in each campaign, as much by guile as by his military strength. Indeed, during the Kumaso campaign, he disguised himself as a maidservant and managed to gain entrance to the palace where the Lord of Kumaso was hosting a drinking party.[15] Once the lord and his guests were thoroughly drunk, he shed his female garments, drew his sword, and mortally wounded the rebel chieftain.[16] On his deathbed, the Lord of Kumaso showed his profound respect for his slayer by renaming him Yamato-takeru, literally the 'Brave One of Yamato', and from that point on it was his only name.[17]

When Yamato-takeru returned to the court in triumph, Keikō feared his son more than ever. So this time he sent him on an even more perilous mission: to subdue the Emeshi, who were almost certainly the indigenous Ainu who lived in the vicinity of what is today Tokyo Bay.[18] Before Yamato-takeru set out, however, his aunt Yamato-no-hime, the 'Princess of Yamato', who was also the high priestess of Amaterasu at the Ise Shrine and the guardian of the Mura-kumo sword, gave the weapon to her nephew, along with some amulets, to help him in his quest.[19] Here again we have the 'Female Sword Bestower'.

Armed with this magical, Excalibur-like sword, Yamato-takeru gained a series of important victories, one of which came close to fulfilling his father's fondest wish. In the course of a battle at Sagami (see Map 5), his enemy set fire to the open grassland on which it was being fought. As his opponent had managed to kill Yamato-takeru's horse, the hero had no means of escaping what appeared to be certain death. But at this critical juncture, the sword magically wielded itself in front of the hero and mowed down the grass that was fuelling the fire. It was this episode that prompted Yamato-takeru to rechristen it Kusanagi no Tsurugi, the 'Grass-Mower Sword',[20] the name it still bears in Japanese literature. Once the fire stopped burning in his direction, the prince used one of the magical amulets his aunt had given him to start a blaze burning in the opposite direction – that is, toward his enemy – and he won the battle handily.

After the grass-burning episode, Yamato-takeru married Miyazu-hime, a princess with whom he'd fallen in love during an earlier expedition.[21] For a time they lived together happily, but the hero had one last task to perform: he had to defeat a monster that lived on a nearby mountain. Ignoring his wife's pleas to take Kusanagi with him, he left the sword in her care, claiming that he could vanquish the creature with his bare hands. That he did, but at a great cost. Soon after his final battle he fell victim to a fatal illness contracted in the struggle. His followers carried the dying hero on a litter to the coast (not unlike Arthur and Batraz), near the modern city of Otsu (See Map 5), where, like all good Japanese warriors, ancient or modern, he died after writing a death poem.[22] Shortly thereafter, his soul turned into a beautiful white bird, which flew off to Yamato; when his tomb was opened, it was empty.

Curiously, the Japanese variant of the embedded-sword story, in which the hero Susanō retrieves a sword from the tail of a dragon, also relates to the Mithraic story, as the dragon in East Asia is equivalent to Taurus in the Western Zodiac.[23] Dragons were also one of the traditional decorations on the kris knife that was invented in Java, Indonesia in the fourteenth century CE, showing that the story spread south as well as east.[24]

There are a number of clear-cut parallels between Yamato-takeru and several Western sword heroes, including the adult Arthur, who received the second Excalibur from a close kinswoman, the Lady of the Lake, and the Ossetic hero Batraz, who, with the help of his aunt, the seeress Satana, received a magical blade from the Divine Smith Kurdalægon.[25] Indeed, the parallel between Batraz and Yamato-takeru in this respect is especially close, as the latter also received his magical sword from *his* aunt, Yamato-no-hime, which suggests that the tale was transmitted by the Alans, the ancestors of the Ossetians and Circassians. To this list we can add Theseus, whose mother, Aethra, showed him the stone under which his father Aegeus had hidden his sword. Thus, the high priestess of Ise is a counterpart of the Lady of the Lake, Satana and Aethra. All four women are Sword Bestowers, and three of them, in addition to being close kinswomen, also possess magical powers.

In this connection, vis-à-vis the Arthurian tradition in particular, the Mura-kumo/Kusanagi is equivalent to *both* of Arthur's swords – the one the young Arthur pulled from the anvil atop a stone and the one he received as an adult from the Lady of the Lake.[26] Indeed, there is a curious inversion between the two sword sagas: Arthur received successively *two* magical swords, while the Kusanagi sword was pulled from an embedded location by one hero and later bestowed by a woman on another.

There are also close parallels between Yamato-takeru and two of the Indo-European sword heroes when it comes to their respective death scenes. Arthur, Batraz and the Japanese hero were each carried to the seashore on litters and died after giving up their magical swords.[27] Both Arthur and Yamato-takeru gave up their magical swords to women, respectively the same kinswoman who initially bestowed it and a beloved wife. Moreover, in all three cases, an emphasis is placed on the way the hero journeys to the afterlife: by barge to a magical afterworld – that is, Avalon – in the case of Arthur, as a spirit rising from the grave in the case of Batraz,[28] and as a giant white bird flying toward his homeland in the case of Yamato-takeru.[29]

To be sure, unlike Arthur and Batraz, neither Theseus nor Yamato-takeru asked that their swords be thrown into the sea as they lay dying, although elements of that motif can in fact also be found elsewhere in East Asian tradition. For instance, the sword, according to some stories, was 'lost at sea after the Imperial Navy was defeated in the Battle of Dan-no-ura in 1185' CE.[30] In a Tang Dynasty tale of the eighth century CE, hero Wu Tzu-hsü threw his magical sword into the Yangtze River. As it entered the water, a dramatic event occurred. Not only did a hand grasp the Chinese hero's sword, as in the *Morte d'Arthur*, but the water became extremely turbulent, and dragons raced back and forth. This, of course, closely parallels what happened when Batraz's sword entered the water – it suddenly turned blood red and stormy.[31]

These parallels among the Indo-European and East Asian sword heroes do not appear to be coincidental. Some years ago, the eminent Japanese historian Namio Egami proposed a still controversial theory that prehistoric Japan was conquered in the late fourth century CE by mounted warriors from the Asian mainland, that is, by what he called the *kiba minzoku*, or 'horse-rider nation',[32] who may have been related to the Alans. According to Egami, Honinigi didn't float down from Heaven, but rather his historical prototype invaded Japan from Korea, securing a beachhead on the southernmost island of Kyushu, from which, several generations later, his descendant, the prototype of Jimmu Tenno, marched eastward and founded the kingdom of Yamato.[33]

That these horse-riders were either far-flung North Iranian cousins of the ancient Scythians or, perhaps more likely, Altaic speakers who had been strongly influenced by one or more such communities[34] is strongly indicated by the parallels between the myth of the three sacred objects sent to earth by Amaterasu and Herodotus' account of the Scythian origin myth in Book IV of the *History*, in which three fiery golden objects – a cup, a battle-ax and a yoked plough – fell from the sky, and were eventually gathered up by Kolaxaïs, the youngest son of the primeval being Targitaos.[35] According to Yoshida,[36] these three sacred Scythian talismans are functional equivalents to the three previously mentioned Japanese talismans: the mirror, the sword and the jewel. Drawing on the famous tripartite Indo-European ideological suggested by the late Georges Dumézil,[37] Yoshida suggests that the cup and the mirror are both reflections of divine sovereignty – that is, of Dumézil's 'first function'. The cup is a sacred, priestly vessel, and it was the mirror that convinced Amaterasu to reassert her sovereignty as sun goddess, while the battle-ax and sword obviously reflect military prowess and belong to the 'second function'; the yoked plough and the *magatama* are intimately connected with fertility, of plants and of human beings respectively, reflecting the 'third function'. In light of these close functional parallels, along with Yoshida, we strongly suspect that the horse riders also introduced the sword hero complex to Japan, including both the embedded and the bestowed sacred sword myths. The story is fracturing in the East as it did in the West as it transmits to new areas and to times when people no longer remember why they are telling it, but the notion that the tale came from the sky is still there, represented by the shift from the Sword in the Stone to the Sword in the Dragon's Tail.

Although there is as yet no clear archaeological evidence for the presence of North Iranian speakers in prehistoric Japan, we can place them on the western border of China around the beginning of the Common Era as an Alanic tribe called the Wo-sun, whose name derives from Oss (as in 'Ossetians)', who paid tribute to the Han Emperor.[38] There were also the Xiongnu, a nomadic steppe people known to the Chinese, who worshipped a sword.[39] Additionally, in the *Samguk Yusa*, the foundation myth of the ancient Korean kingdom of Silla, there is an account of three sacred objects descending from the sky, which reinforces the theory that the prototype of Honinigi and his Indo-European-type mounted war-band, the prototype of the historical Samurai order, almost certainly passed through Korea en route to Japan *c.* 400 CE.

Nor should we forget that the Huns also practised sword worship,[40] and the description of their ceremony matches the 'Scythian Ares' description by Herodotus (see chapter 5).[41] By the time the story of this sword, Ching-lu, gets to Atilla the Hun, the blade is both a sword and a god, a weapon would help him conquer the world.

Weapons of Iron

Slightly earlier than the time the flanged-tang sword appeared in Greece (*c.* 1250–1200 BCE), an iron sword was manufactured in China (*c.* 1500 BCE).[42] Around the time of the Roman emperor Augustus, the Chinese shifted from making swords out of iron to fashioning them out of steel.[43] But the original sword was of iron. The knowledge of ironworking could easily have been transmitted from the Eurasian steppes to China by the same nomads who transmitted the knowledge to the Hittites.

Although it is not directly related to either the Susanō or Yamato-takeru stories, there is yet another motif unique to the Ossetic Nart Sagas and ancient Japanese mythology and folklore that reinforces this suggested connection between Japan and the ancient North Iranians. This is the motif of the 'Metaled Man', which we've seen in several of the sword stories. For instance, at Satana's urging, the infant Batraz is encased in metal by Divine Smith Kurdalægon and is thus rendered invulnerable.[44] A close parallel can be seen in the Japanese legend of Tetsu-jin, or 'Iron Man', a morally ambivalent semi-trickster – like Batraz, if not Yamato-takeru – who is also encased in iron and thus invulnerable, save for his eyes.[45]

Variations of the motif also appear the stories of Achilles, who, as an infant, is dipped by his mother in the River Styx and thereby rendered invulnerable, save for the heel by which she held him; and Siegfried, who bathes in Fafnir's blood and also becomes invulnerable to weapons except for the spot on his shoulder where a laurel leaf lands. But neither of these figures is encased in iron, which leads us to believe that the basic motif here is extremely ancient and predates the spread of iron technology from north-east Anatolia/Transcaucasia in the late second millennium BCE. Again, the similarities are too specific to be explained by recourse to independent invention.

We have now arrived at the point where we can draw together these scattered parts of the great story told in the heavens and in so doing show how this single strand, for all its variants, remained true to something observed by our ancestors 42,000 years ago.

PART V

THE SWORD IN THE STARS

9

ZODIACAL LORE AND LEGEND

Having surveyed the many and widely differing aspects of the Sword in the Stone tale, it is time to draw together the many strands of the pattern which emerges and to see just how it represents an ancient movement within the cosmos that was felt deeply enough to introduce a new story into the collective mythology of the world.

To begin our understanding of this we need to look back to the moment when the Zodiac as we know it was conceptualised, roughly 4,000 years ago in *c.* 2,000 BCE.[1] Long before GPS locators and when ambient light from cities had not yet blotted out all but the brightest objects in the night sky, our ancestors stared up at the celestial river of the Milky Way and the stars and planets to either side of it and tried to play 'connect the dots'. These images became the constellations, many of which are associated with myths that attempted to explain phenomena observed in the sky. Anyone checking the earliest efforts to navigate by the stars

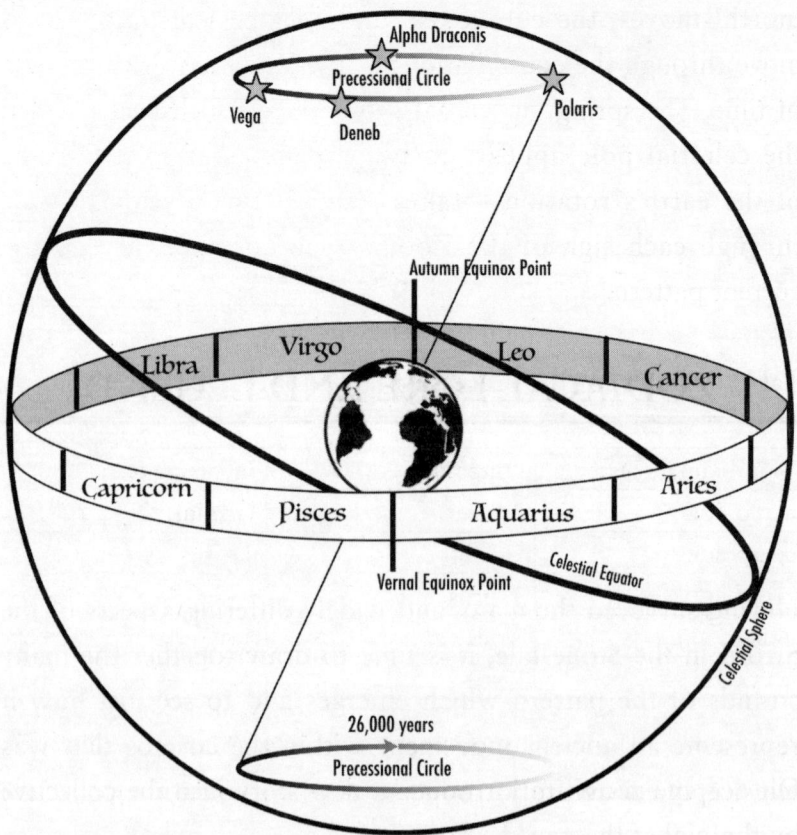

Fig. 4. The Precession of the Equinoxes. (W. Kinghan)

in the Northern Hemisphere, whether on an actual sea or a sea of grass, cannot help but notice that something terrifying happens over the course of centuries: north, and with it the pole star, moves. This movement is caused by the gravitational pull exerted on the earth by the sun and moon, by the not-quite-spherical shape of the earth, and by the tilt of the earth's axis. The earth 'wobbles' as it rotates, and the apparent spot around which the earth spins appears to shift. Northshift is not random, but follows a 25,920-year cycle, which is also known as the 'precession of the equinoxes'.[2] This is because, just as 'north' moves, the equinoxes (and solstices) also appear to move through the constellations of the Zodiac over the course of time. The spring, or 'vernal', equinox – which occurs when the celestial pole appears to be perpendicular to the access of the earth's rotation – takes roughly 2,160 years to pass through each sign of the Zodiac.[3] For instance, here is the current pattern.

Table 6. Dates for the Precession of the Spring Equinox[4]

Approximate Date	Outgoing Sign	Incoming Sign
6480 BCE	Cancer	Gemini
4320 BCE	Gemini	Taurus
2160 BCE	Taurus	Aries
6 BCE	Aries	Pisces
2154 CE	Pisces	Aquarius

One of the most important pieces of information provided by the night sky was the position of travellers when orienting themselves to north, south, east and west. Anyone attempting to navigate by the stars usually does so by locating the pole star.[5] Even today, many of us teach our children how to find the Great Bear in Ursa Major and follow it to where an imaginary line meets at the pole star in Ursa Minor.[6] That lesson, however, usually comes with a huge piece of misinformation. The pole star does *not* indicate true north. What the ancient civilisations of Eurasia noticed was that the north moves. While the pole star is said to mark true north, it has nothing to do with the earth's magnetic pole, the one that we think of as passing from the Arctic to the Antarctic. The wobble in the earth's spin causes a tilt in the earth's axis.

What we are actually spinning around is something referred to as the *celestial* pole. It takes roughly 25,772 (25,920) years for the celestial pole to return to the point where it appears to have started. Meanwhile, 'north' seems to travel through the constellations of what eventually became known as the Zodiac.

The 'world pillars' are the constellations in which the sun rises at the solstices and equinoxes,[7] and it is between these pillars that the celestial pole passes. Also called 'The Nail of the Heavens', this is used as a fixed point in navigation throughout the Western Hemisphere. At any given point in time, these constellations, together with the celestial pole, which we argue can be a sword or a tree, figure in ancient stories that describe this Northshift.

For example, *c.* 2500 BCE, Thuban in the constellation Draco was the pole star.[8] In other words, the 'sword' used to be in Draco's tail in the West. Coincidentally, it will later wind up in the Eastern Zodiac's Dragon's Tail in China and Japan during the next shift. The Delphic story of Pytho the Dragon, 'presumably the constellation traditionally named Draco ... is told from a camera angle focused specifically on Northshift rather than on Precession, suggesting a local tradition that developed before the diffusion of the Near Eastern model known as 'the Kingship in Heaven'.[9] In *c.* 500 CE, Polaris, in the constellation Ursa Minor, became the pole star, and about 13,000 years from now Vega, in the constellation Lyra, will become the pole star.[10] In between times, when there is an observable pole star, the position of the celestial pole can be determined by noting the positions of the various constellations around it.

Table 7. Dates of Northshift[11]

Precessional Constellation (Summer Solstice)	Libra	Virgo	Leo	Cancer
Precessional Constellation (Winter Solstice)	Aries	Pisces	Aquarius	Capricorn
Precessional Constellation (Spring Equinox)	Cancer	Gemini	Taurus	Aries
Precessional Constellation (Summer Equinox)	Capricorn	Sagittarius	Scorpio	Libra
Polar Star			Thuban	
Approximate date of shift	8640 BCE	6480 BCE	4320 BCE	2160 BCE

Before the creation of the Zodiac regularised things, stories tracked the movement in the stars with respect to the constellations that marked the equinoxes and the solstices. All the Babylonians did was shift the focus to the stars, as some peoples like the Hittites had already started to do, and codify them. This movement, called the precession of the equinoxes, reveals incremental changes within the heavens in relation to the earth. Thus, *c.* 12,000 BCE, Vega in the constellation Lyra was the pole star. Then Thuban in the constellation Draco moved into its place *c.* 2500 BCE.[12] In 2140 BCE, Polaris, which is in Ursa Minor (the Little Dipper), became the new pole star. Deneb, in the constellation Cygnus, will become the pole star in *c.* 11,000 CE and in approximately 15,000 CE Vega in the constellation Lyra will become the pole star once again.[13]

Table 8. Northshift[14]

Precessional Constellation (Summer Solstice)	Libra	Virgo	Leo	Cancer
Precessional Constellation (Winter Solstice)	Aries	Pisces	Aquarius	Capricorn
Precessional Constellation (Spring Equinox)	Cancer	Gemini	Taurus	Aries
Precessional Constellation (Summer Equinox)	Capricorn	Sagittarius	Scorpio	Libra
Polar Star			Thuban	
Approximate date of shift	8640 BCE	6480 BCE	4320 BCE	2160 BCE

The focus on things regarded as most important to the people who observed them accompanied these shifts. For instance, when the precession occurred *c.* 6480 BCE, the emphasis in the stories was on the shift of the summer solstice from Libra into Virgo, which indicates that the constellations already had an established presence, even though the Zodiac had yet to be organised as such.

Depending on the hemisphere and latitude, different stars, some moving and some not, were visible in a variety of positions. The ones important to this discussion are seen from the Northern Hemisphere, roughly between the 30th and 60th latitude. Above these latitudes the constellations important to these stories are not visible, and tales outside that band were carried outward from somewhere within it to areas like Sweden, Japan and Africa. The farther the tale transmits from the point of origin, the more the details are scattered and subject to variation.

The clear skies of the Middle East provided a perfect opportunity for the observation of the heavens. Following the movement of the sword myth, we arrive at the great Sumerian civilisations and their decedents. The Sumerians settled in Mesopotamia *c.* 5500–4000 BCE. They were a West Asian people who spoke a non-Indo-European and non-Semitic language. The Mesopotamian civilisation, which followed the Babylonian, had developed a sophisticated astronomical understanding as early as 2000 BCE. They had already recognised and named the planets, and their general knowledge of the stars preceded Western astrology with its identification of planets with deities and mythical beings. The height of the Sumerian civilisation in Mesopotamia was *c.* 2334–2154 BCE.

Next came the Babylonians, who settled between the Tigris and Euphrates rivers in Mesopotamia and were an Akkadian-speaking people from the Semitic cultures. Eventually their language became a mix of Sumerian and Akkadian, as did their religion, as they absorbed the people around them. They are credited with development of the mathematical precision of the Zodiac post 700 BCE, but other peoples were already noting and telling stories about the constellations they saw in the stars by at least 2000 BCE, if not earlier. The Sumerians fell to the Babylonians *c.* 1700 BCE, but before that they were neighbours to the Hittites, who had the sword god who presided over the spring equinox.

The Hittites came to Anatolia from the south Russian steppes and established their kingdom *c.* 1650 BCE, but they had already moved out of the steppes by 2230 BCE.[15] As we saw in chapter 1, in 2160 BCE the celestial pole shifted from Taurus into Aries, the two signs presided over by the Hittite sword god, and before that it passed from Gemini into Taurus, an event also recorded in the Hittite (or Hurrian) pantheon. The Scythian sword god, as we noted, was only associated with the sign of Aries, represented by the story of the ram, which featured in the story of Jason. The twelve figures associated with the sword god in Yazılıkaya, then, may have nothing at all to do with Underworld deities. Instead, they may represent the twelve signs of the Zodiac, and the crossroads the Hittites associated with them might not be underground at all, but rather in the sky.

This Hittite version of the sword god has several elements in common with the Arthurian variant and several of the other stories we've explored. They feature a sword in a graveyard. The swords are associated with a king. The twelve runners in the Hittite variant parallel the Twelve Knights of the Round Table in Arthurian tradition and the Twelve Companions of Charlemagne. Also, the anvil of the Arthurian variant preserves the connection between the forging of iron, which we have seen throughout as playing an important part in the development and transmission of the myth. These tales are clearly part of the same tradition, yet, by placing the image of the sword god in conjunction with celestial deities at Yazılıkaya, the Hittites retained an association that the Arthurian variant lost: the tale of the Sword in the Stone had something to do with the stars.

The Divine Warrior, represented by Ares, took his sword and stabbed it across the circle of the Zodiac, embedding his weapon in the opposite sign. For the Hittites, the opposite sign would have been a stone altar in the sign of Libra. So when the story travelled south from the steppes, the older image of the sword planted in a wooden altar became a sword planted in a stone while the shift of focus from the altar to the pole wound up planting the sword in a tree.

Astronomical tablets from the Babylonian period reveal their sophistication; they knew that these constellations were important – as was the precession of the equinoxes. When the shift occurred again *c.* 4320 BCE, the focus changed from the summer solstice to the spring equinox and the 'Kingship in Heaven' theme, which dealt with the transference of power from one leader to another, was added to the myth. This characterised the movement of the equinox from Gemini to Taurus. In other words, the fact that the celestial pole was perpendicular to the sun became more important than the day being the longest of the year. This may be because Thuban, which is located in the constellation Draco in the region dominated by Virgo (the outgoing sign), became the pole star. The story of the 'Kingship in Heaven' then continued when the spring equinox shifted from Taurus into Aries in 2160 BCE, with the focus now on the pole, which represented the World Tree[16] for the Germanic peoples.

The precession of the pole star in the constellations prefigures a change in mythology. Here is the pattern.

Table 9. Pole Stars

Pole Star	Constellation	Approximate Date
Vega	Lyra	12000 BCE
Thuban	Draco	2500 BCE
Polaris	Ursa Minor	2140 BCE
Deneb	Cygnus	11000 CE
Vega	Lyra	15000 CE

When the pole shifted from Taurus into Aries we got Mithras attacking the bull. Then the shift from Aries to Pisces corresponded to the rise of Christianity in the first century CE, and this was reflected in the symbology of the time. Thus, in the period from 2160 BCE to 6 BCE, under the rule of Aries, we see the Ram of Egypt, the story of Abraham's sacrifice of the lamb, etc. Then, between 6 BCE and 2154 CE in Pisces, we find the Christian symbol of the fish (*Icthys*), Jesus multiplying fish and having twelve disciples. The next precessional sign, Aquarius (the actual age of Aquarius, not the much-touted Aquarian Age of recent times), will involve myths and emblems of water. Yet during the shift before that, *c.* 2140 BCE, when Polaris became the Pole Star, is when the sword god reigned, and the images were of the embedded sword.[17]

Migrating Traditions

We know of at least two themes that the ancients used to describe these astronomical events. One is 'the Kingship in Heaven', whereby one god or pantheon is replaced by its successor, and the other sits at the heart of the cult of Mithras, where the slaying of the bull reflects the movement from Taurus to Aries. In this book we have proposed that there was also a third theme that carried details of these heavenly events: the story of the Sword in the Stone.

Folk narratives can be generated in one of two ways. The first, 'monogenesis', means that the story has a single point of origin and spreads out, or 'diffuses', from its single source. This is very typical of complicated tales, stories that have several distinctive motifs, that are strung together in a specific way. The second is 'polygenesis'. This means that multiple sources come up with the same tale at multiple places and in multiple times with no physical point of connection among them. The odds of multiple cultures producing nearly identical versions of a tale decrease as the story increases in complexity and the consistency of what it represents. The odds of independent invention become even more vast if such narratives refer to a specific event by way of explaining or trying to make sense out of what happened in a certain manner. The vision of the firmament, despite variants of locale and culture, is common to all the examples of the embedded-sword motif that we have examined.

As we discussed in the introduction, to work out how a story was transmitted, folklorists employ the 'historic-geographic method', either in its original or modified form. This system of analysis, developed by the great folklorists Antti Aarne and Stith Thompson,[18] is based upon the idea of collecting all known variants of a tale and plotting on a map the written ones (as well as the visual and plastic arts) by date of creation and the oral ones by date of collection. By analysing the results, the researcher can get at least a general idea about where a complicated story developed and how it spread.[19] This method, when used incautiously, has led to some grand mistakes over the centuries.[20] Judicious application, however, has yielded entire fields of study, such as that of Indo-European Comparative Mythology, which proposes that members of the Indo-European family of languages share certain stories, mythological and otherwise, that were transmitted to their Indo-European descendants.

Of the various forms of folklore, the one that is hardest to transmit is legend. This is because legend is tied to a specific historic event or character, at a specific place and a specific time. We often understand the stories better in context locally.

The moment those factors become unintelligible to the audience, the story ceases to transmit – or updates to a form that *is* intelligible to the audience. When a legend, however, becomes translated into a myth,[21] the religious factor increases not only the longevity of the story but also makes it harder for the story to be transmitted across language barriers, because the transmitter and recipient do not have a common linguistic and/or cultural frame of reference. In other words, transmission is more difficult to an 'outside' culture – unless there is something that boosts its power and thus the influence of the story, which then becomes universally applicable. This is what we think happened in the case of the Sword in the Stone, since we have examples of diffusion to non-Indo-European cultures, which underscores that the tale was not a result of parallel development.

There was more than one way to tell stories about the phenomenon of Northshift, and most of these we have explored in this book. If we look again at some of these, in conjunction with the movement of the stars, we see that while the stories of generations of gods overthrown by their children began by focusing on the precession of the summer solstice, the focus changed to the precession of the spring equinox and of the celestial pole, engendering another set of stories that described changes in the kingdom of heaven, namely the incoming sign of the Zodiac attacking the outgoing sign. These actions are identified in the tales of Mithras.

Here we see that Mithras plunging his sword into the neck of a bull reflects both an annual sacrifice usually conducted in the context of the winter solstice, and a similar event that took place on 24 March, intended to encourage the sun to leave Taurus at the spring equinox. He does this surrounded by representations of the constellations of the Zodiac, including a ram that is attacking the bull. Both versions of the ceremony – known as the *taurobolium*, a priest portraying Mithras as a virile young warrior deity with strong solar associations, slew a black bull that represented darkness, thus ensuring the rebirth of what the Romans called Sol Invictus, the 'Unconquered Sun'.

Recent researchers have recognised a host of more complex astral symbols in the *taurobolium* (or *tauroctony*, as the ceremony was also sometimes called). Ulansey detailed the celestial imagery of the Mithraic cult as linked to the phenomenon of the precession.[22] It is quite clear from contemporary imagery of the warrior slaying the bull, which includes a scorpion and serpent attacking from below and a dog lapping up the bull's blood, that the myths carried information taken from the constellations.

The artists who created the imagery of the cult were not subtle about the connection: most Mithraic images include the sun, moon and stars. In the worship of Mithras, we have the warrior stabbing the bull, in other words Aries attacking the adjacent sign of Taurus.[23] Jason's is a similar tale. In the story of the Argonauts, we see that, beginning at the isle of Lemnos off the coast of Anatolia (Turkey), a group of assorted demigods and heroes led by Jason take part in a number of adventures, most of which are not to their credit. They pass beyond Bear Mountain, encountering the people of Thrace. They pass through Clashing Rocks that they force to join into one, then sail over the Black Sea to Georgia. In order to win the Golden Fleece, Jason enlists the help of Medea help to plough a field with fire-breathing oxen (possibly Taurus) and sow the field with dragon's teeth (possibly Draco) from which warriors spring up. Jason defeats them by throwing a rock into their midst (possibly Libra), which causes them to kill each other. Then Jason steals the Golden Fleece (Aries) from the dragon (Draco) and escapes with Medea. Note that this story appears in an area near the 44th parallel north and involves the same constellations that appear in later stories, including those of the steppe nomads. As we have noted, a similar story is told in reverse among the steppe peoples who transmit the Nart Sagas, signalling that the people doing the storytelling were aware that the stories were transmitting in two directions yet talking about the same thing.

The other famous Hellenic myth, concerning the hero Theseus and his most infamous opponent, the Minotaur, a 'form of the Cretan bull-god',[24] as we saw suggests a further reference to Taurus. Again, we have a virile young warrior who, in this instance, uses a sword recovered from beneath a stone to slay a taurine creature – thus clearing the decks, as it were, for a new age.[25] Could this famous tale reflect the *same* equinoctial precession reflected in the *taurobolium*? Like Mithras' immolation of the celestial bull, Theseus' encounter with the Minotaur occurred deep underground[26] and Theseus is attached to the outside world by a golden thread, recalling Zeus' golden rope, which was provided for him by a woman, in this case Ariadne. The thread is suggestive of the story of the Golden Fleece, which ties Theseus to the sign of Aries, making him the Divine Warrior who slays, or conquers, the bull.

Ironically, awareness of the imminence of the next precession – or Northshift – from Aries into Pisces, at *c.* 6 BC, seems to have played a major part in the spread of the *taurobolium* of Mithras throughout the Roman Empire shortly before the beginning of the Common Era. The basic idea of a precession cycle was worked out by the Greek astronomer Hipparchos around 128 BCE[27] and it is probably not a coincidence that the westward diffusion of the Mithraic cult began shortly after Hipparchos' death in *c.* 120 BCE. It would appear that the prospect of a new shift, this time from Aries into Pieces, prompted people to hearken back to the symbolism of the previous one, that is, the Taurus-to-Aries shift in 2150 BCE.

We believe that the combination of this religious symbolism with the astronomical observations and the development and distribution of the knowledge of how to forge iron account for the distribution of the Sword in the Stone story throughout much of Eurasia and into parts of Africa and from there into the Americas. Note that the narrative was not limited to the Indo-European family of languages and that the majority of the variants were collected roughly between the 40th and 60th parallel north, east of the Mediterranean Sea. It was clearly carrying something important that people were supposed to know regarding something that was happening in the sky around 2200 BCE. We think that information was the precession of the equinoxes.

In the Germanic cultures, the pole was the World Tree, Yggdrasil, which is represented in the *Volsunga Saga* by the Branstock, a great tree used by King Volsung to act as the central pillar of his mighty hall. This, as we saw, is a variant Sword in the Stone story, when the god Odin arrives in the hall and embeds a mighty sword deep into the Branstock. A tree appears in some retellings of Northshift story because the celestial pole is both the World Tree and the sword, which is why the sword is in the tree in the Germanic tradition.[28] The celestial pole itself, situated at the centre of the heavens, is depicted as many different things, from a spindle to a churn. In the nomadic cultures of Eurasia, the pole was sometimes represented by a tent pole but, as we have shown, we believe it could also be a sword.[29] Also, this variant of the story only transmits from the Eurasian Culture Complex. Cultures as far removed from the steppes as the Maya and the ancient Polynesians were also aware of Northshift, but they did not use the story of the Sword in the Stone to describe it.[30]

While Mithras attacks the Zodiacal sign Taurus, which the celestial pole is leaving, the hero in the Sword in the Stone story wields the pole itself, in this case the sword, that he sticks into or pulls out of the opposite sign. In 2150 BCE the sign was Libra. It did not become a set of scales until the Romans decided to reinstate the symbolism of the old Babylonian layout of the heavens. The stone altar, however, was always a part of the constellation. Agreeing with some of the ideas stated by the Barbers in their ground-breaking book *When they Severed Earth from Sky*, we think that the Sword in the Stone story started out as a myth about the precession of the celestial pole from Taurus into Aries in 2140 BCE, which was represented in the image of the Hittite sword god. Absolutely none of these stories or images are found prior to 2160 CE.

According to Germanicus Caesar, to whom the authorship of an astrological text known as the *Aratus* is sometimes ascribed, the cycle for Aries is the same length as that of Ursa Major, and he singles out Aries, the Claws (Libra) and Orion's Belt as being particularly close to the celestial pole. He knew Libra as both 'the Altar' (part of Scorpio separated into a southern constellation) and 'the Claws' of Scorpio.[31] The Altar is so far south that it barely rises above the latitudes from which it is visible where the story of the Sword in the Stone was told. These celestial phenomena were thought of by the ancients as belonging together, while the Sword in the Stone narratives suggest that there once existed a tale describing how the warrior associated with Aries stabbed a sword across the Zodiac, passed the Bears and the star Arcturus, and plunged it into the stone Altar associated with Libra.

Mithras' sword is one of many embedded blades that reflect this phenomenon. Indeed, the Mithraic version is in many respects an expression of this steppe-rooted tradition, as it not only involves a young warrior heroically embedding (and, one must presume, later retrieving) a sword, but it also, as we have seen, reflects the specific Zodiacal symbolism of the 'death' of Taurus and the shift into a sign (Aries) that is clearly associated with war and youthful warriors, such as the story Jason and his quest for the Golden Fleece, which has Aries symbolism written all over it.

The most famous example of the Sword in the Stone is, of course, King Arthur's first sword, which signifies the emergence of a triumphant king. To be sure, a bull plays no part in the Arthurian variant; it does, however, appear in the Scythian practice of embedding swords in brush piles, collecting blood from slaughtered cattle (or sometimes defeated warriors) in a golden cup, and pouring it over the sword.[32] This theme also reappears in Irish myth, and was still known as late as the seventeenth century.[33] In fact, all of these embedded-sword stories ultimately lead us back to the steppes, and the story of Arthur's sword was almost certainly brought to Britain by the Alans' western cousins, a *numerus* of Sarmatians posted there by Marcus Aurelius in 175 CE,[34] while the Alans themselves likely brought it to Burgundy, where Robert de Boron wrote his *Merlin*.

So, when ancient cultures wanted to pass critical information on to future generations, they placed it in a story, used as a mnemonic – one that was so compelling that people would remember the information contained therein when it was needed. What these nomadic cultures came up with was a story about a sword in a stone and anvil, sometimes in a graveyard, which everyone at the time knew was a representation of the Heavens and the Zodiac.[35]

Alas, as the saying goes, 'Stories don't move – people do.' This applies in space as well as in time, and the purpose behind this story became lost over the millennia. The closer you are to the steppes, the point of origin for the tale, or to large settlements of steppe nomads, the more details from the original story are in the local variant. That is why the anvil variant is found north of the Caucasus Mountains.

Around 2160 BCE, triggered by the Northshift, a story about a sacred bronze sword plunging into a tree (or brush pile) emerged among the ancient steppe peoples. When that story transmitted to the Near East, a stone throne or altar was added to the tale. With the development of forging iron, the sword became iron instead of bronze. The Near Eastern variants, such as that among the Hittites, lost the element of the wood/tree and retained the stone. As the tale spread north with the Scythians, the variant with the sword in the altar atop the brush pile developed by 400 BCE. The Alans stayed in the Caucasus region, trading with the Near East, and picked up the variant without the wood. The Sarmatians absorbed the Royal Scythians and picked up the variant with the wood. The Sarmatians then transmitted the variant with the wood to the Germanic peoples who, because of their own World Tree story, picked up a doublet version of the tale, one with the sword in the tree and another with the sword cutting through stone and iron, which eventually became combined into a single tale. The variant of the story that surfaced in the medieval Arthurian legends came to Europe later and through a different agency than the Germanic stories, but both traditions of the embedded sword ultimately stem from the same tale. The story also spread to Japan, Sweden and Yorubaland, likely through the agency of horse-riding nomads. As these horse-riding warriors came into contact with other cultures and transmitted their knowledge of forging iron, they also transmitted stories about the deity who oversaw both war and smithing.

Forging Iron and Sword Gods

We have seen how the knowledge of ironworking first appeared in the 'second half of the third millennium B.C. in Anatolia'.[36] Milisauskas noted that the Scythian influence in Celtic art of the La Tène period could have come in with iron technology, and this agrees with what we find in the patterns of transmission for the tale of the Sword in the Stone.[37] Knowledge of ironworking first appeared c. 600–300 BCE among Germanic peoples in the area of the Jastorf culture, south of the Elbe and north of the Weser.[38] This was not, however, forging swords. The Germanic peoples did not start forging iron into longer swords intended for use by cavalry until the Late Roman Iron Age, c. 180–400 CE.[39]

The Kalybes were probably responsible for the addition of the anvil and other ironworking pieces of the tale, though we suspect the steppe cultures were responsible for the distribution of that set of motifs because only in the steppe cultures did the sword god, rather than the Divine Smith, wind up in charge of ironworking. The overall distribution of the tale matches the pattern of the steppe cultures spreading south, west and east out of the steppes.

To sum up, thanks to a celestial event witnessed in Transcaucasia in the late third millennium BCE, both the embedded and received sword traditions, plus those concerning the heroes that wield them and the 'magic ladies' who bestow them, have managed to traverse the Old World, from Japan to West Africa and from there to the Americas. It appeared most notably in the Arthurian legends. Only by looking back through the centuries, and turning our eyes to the heavens, do we see how these disparate elements were connected into an ancient star-myth which saw to it that the story remained in the consciousness of the widespread cultural areas we have explored here, and that it remained at the heart of Western mythology ever since.

Appendix I

ARTHUR AND THE VOYAGE NORTH

In an essay published in 1881 by the American writer Benjamin Franklin Decosta exploring the evidence for early arctic exploration, we find this wonderful phrase: 'Nature appears partial towards the North.' He continues from this statement:

> The equator heat is by no means coincident with the equatorial line. In portions of the Pacific the equator heat indeed runs south of the geographical equator, but elsewhere it sweeps 210 degrees north of the line, and from thence hot waves are thrown off towards the pole. When battling his way towards the higher latitudes, man acts in sympathy with the mightiest forces of nature. The magnetic needle, pointing steadfastly towards the north, is the index of his mind...[1]

Even this late on, the northern wastes were somehow seen as mysterious in a way that reaches back to the earliest accounts of voyages undertaken to explore the furthest reaches of the world. It comes to something of a head in the later part of the sixteenth century, which saw a period of intense exploration of the world by the great sea captains of the age that has seldom been equalled.

Many of these early navigators were not so much interested in exploration as in the acquiring of new territories, and this is especially true of Britain and her arch-rival, Spain. Between 1495 and 1530 Britain sent explorers westward in search of a New World, with the result that John and Sebastian Cabot, among others, claimed Newfoundland and portions of North America along the Atlantic seaboard for Henry VII and his successors. In the 1550s, pilots working for the Muscovy Trading Company, such as Richard Chancellor and Stephen Borough, travelled north-east in search of new opportunities for trade. But it was not until 1576, when Martin Frobisher set out in search of a north-west passage believed to connect the Atlantic and Pacific oceans, that serious plans for the New World began to take shape. Within a few years, Frobisher conducted two additional exploratory voyages, and, along with Humphrey Gilbert, was authorised by the Crown to settle permanent colonies in the North Atlantic. It was at this time that Francis Drake undertook his circumnavigation of the world.

During this intense period of English overseas expansionism, many important questions were asked. What did the geography of the Northern Hemisphere look like? Should Frobisher be seeking a north-west or a north-east passage? Were Drake's and Frobisher's activities legal? What rights do the English have to lands in the North Atlantic in North America? How could English activity in these regions be justified to the Spanish and Portuguese, who also claimed legal rights to these regions? These questions emerged during a sensitive time in the relations between Protestant England and Catholic Europe, and more particularly between England and Spain. A few false steps in the direction of North America could lead to war.

But one man set out to answer some of these questions, while at the same time making his mark at court and becoming a favourite of Queen Elizabeth. This was John Dee, and during this period he was often called to court to advise on decisions about England's nascent empire.

Thanks to his expertise in astrology, not to mention his reported conversations with angels, Dee found great favour with Queen Elizabeth. At this time he travelled to Holland and met the famous cartographer Gerardus Mercator. The two men became good friends and when Dee returned to England in 1551 he brought with him a valuable collection of mathematical and astronomical instruments, including one of Mercator's globes. His interest in geography began from this time and was to become particularly important later on during his years of service to Queen Elizabeth I.[2]

Dee began to explore two new avenues of knowledge. The first involved the geographical expansion of Queen Elizabeth's British Empire – a term that Dee himself coined. It was at this time that he began to use the term, bringing it into common usage.

Dee also began to advise the leading explorers of the day, providing maps and charts (many at least half-imaginary) that would enable them to claim more lands for the queen. At the same time he worked his way though hundreds of supposedly historical documents, seeking evidence that lands once ruled over by Elizabeth's predecessors were still rightly hers.

In 1577 he published *General and Rare Memorials Pertayning to the Perfect Arte of Navigation*, a work that set out his vision of a maritime empire and asserted English territorial claims over the New World.[3] This was in part to promote Frobisher's voyage and the trading goals of the Muscovy Company. It was published in a limited run of 100 copies in 1577. It is very possible that the queen herself suppressed its wider distribution because she was interested in keeping secret many of the ideas expressed within. In a highly symbolic frontispiece, the book depicted the figure of Britannia kneeling by the shore, beseeching Queen Elizabeth to protect her empire by strengthening her navy.

This was followed in 1578 by *The Limits of the British Empire* in which, using the eleventh-century pseudo-history *Historia regum Britanniae* by Geoffrey of Monmouth, Dee argued that because King Arthur had extended his kingdom to include Ireland, Greenland, Iceland and parts of the North Pole, so too might the queen. He argued also that England should garner new lands through colonisation and that this vision could become reality by way of maritime supremacy.[4]

In fact, the book is more of a miscellany of earlier works, all revolving around the idea that England's queen had the rights to rule over territories to the north. The reason given was that the renowned King Arthur has conquered these lands in the sixth century and that since this conquest had never been challenged it still held true. The fact that the court considered this argument important is indicated by the detail that in 1593 the book was recorded as being in the library of William Cecil, Lord Burghley, Elizabeth's chief minister. Burghley himself made a note headed 'A summary of Mr. Dees book', which contains a brief statement of the parts of the text that relate to the Arthurian conquest of the north.[5]

Dee certainly discussed the ideas expressed in the manuscript with the queen. In his diary he records that between 22 and 28 November 1577 he travelled to Windsor and had three meetings with Elizabeth and her spymaster, Francis Walsingham, during which he 'declared to the Queen her title to Greenland, Estotiland [a contested location, possibly Labrador] and Friesland'.[6]

The book's aim is simple – to gather evidence supporting the idea that Her Majesty could lay legitimate claim not only to Britain, Scotland, Wales and Ireland but also Norway, Sweden, Iceland, Greenland, possibly the continent of America, and regions even further north – as far, in fact, as the North Polar ice itself. In the process Dee told a story about the renowned King Arthur that appears nowhere else, and is very startling indeed.

At the beginning of the book Dee writes:

Because the promised records ensuing depend chiefly upon our King Arthur and his wonderful foreign conquest, I think it not impertinent first to say a word or two about our worthy prince, who for his chivalrous excellence with sundry foreign Christian nations (by their common consent) is recorded one of the nine most valiant captains that have ever been since the world began.[7]

This is a reference to Arthur being numbered among the Nine Worthies, heroes who were considered of tremendous importance. They comprised three pagans (Hector of Troy, Alexander the Great and Julius Caesar), three Jews (Joshua, David and Judas Maccabeus), and three Christians (King Arthur, Charlemagne and Godfrey of Bouillon).

Dee continues with a broad summary of Arthur's life and conflicts with the Saxons, Picts and Scots that is based, for the most part, on the work of Geoffrey of Monmouth. Dee is surprisingly accurate here, dating Arthur to the sixth century and mentioning the twelve famous battles against the Saxons at a time when most people would have described him as a medieval king ruling over a largely legendary kingdom. The fact that he is unaware that Arthur was never a king, only receiving his crown at the hands of later medieval writers, does not affect his central idea.

Having stated his intent, Dee wastes no time in getting to the point with an altogether more startling account, describing how Arthur subdued Norway, Iceland, Greenland, Finland, Lapland and 'all the other lands and Islands of the East Sea, even unto Russia ... even unto the North Pole'. He adds, curiously, that the people in these areas are wild and savage, 'because *all evil comes from the North*, yet there were among them certain Christians living in secret' [italics ours].[8]

'Even unto the North Pole.' There is the statement that leaps out at us. Never mind that Arthur is seen as conquering most of present-day Scandinavia, parts of Russia and possibly even parts of America and Canada, here he travels into the deepest north. Where did Dee get this from?

Always a precise and energetic researcher, he began by looking at what was then considered the most reliable account of King Arthur: the aforementioned *Historia regum Britanniae*. There he found the following passage:

As soon as the next summer came around, Arthur fitted out a fleet and sailed off to the island of Ireland, which he was determined to subject to his own authority ... Arthur then steered his fleet to Iceland, defeated the people there and subdued the island. A rumour spread through all the other islands that no country could resist Arthur. Doldavius, King of Gotland, Gunhpa, King of the Orkneys, came of their own free will to promise tribute and do homage ... the fact that [Arthur] was dreaded by all encouraged him to conceive the idea of conquering the whole of Europe. He fitted out his fleets and sailed first of all to Norway ... [His soldiers] scattered the rural population and continued to give full license to their savagery until they had forced all Norway and all Denmark too, to accept Arthur's rule.[9]

According to Geoffrey, Arthur's conquest did not stop here. He marched on Gaul and conquered it and finally came as far as the walls of Rome. Here Arthur is no longer seen as an insular war leader but instead as an Emperor of the West. But this is still only part of Dee's desire – which was to prove Arthur the conqueror of the northern world.

In his book, Dee now goes on to discuss other documents that he had found, which proved Arthur's journey to the north and his eventual rule over not only the northern countries but beyond – to the very region of the Arctic itself.

The story of how this came about is complicated, requiring a look back to the twelfth century, and in particular to a book known by the title *Gestae Arthuri* (Deeds of Arthur). Unfortunately this book no longer exists, or is currently lost in the depths of some library, awaiting rediscovery. As with many classical texts, however, fragments were quoted in later works, including the writings of the explorer Richard Hakluyt, who made a translation of part of it in his book *Principal Navigations*.

It was to his friend the explorer and cartographer Mercator that Dee turned for a fuller description. Mercator himself had inscribed his great wall-map of 1569 CE with the following account:

Touching the description of the North parts, I have taken the same part of the voyages of James Cnoyen of Hartzevan Buske, which allegeth certain conquest of King Arthur of Britain ... and chiefest things among the rest he learned [from] a certain priest in the King of Norway's Court in the year 1364. This priest was descended (in the fifth generation) from [those whom] King Arthur had sent to inhabit these islands... [10]

'These islands' included Greenland, Estotiland, Iceland and so on. Clearly excited by this, Dee enquired of his friend the source of this statement. Mercator replied that he had made notes from a manuscript of the said James Cnoyen, a noted Dutch traveller: 'The idea about the northern regions which some time ago I extracted from him, follow [him] Word for Word save where for the sake of brevity or speed I have translated into Latin, when if not always his words I have retained his meaning.'[11] He then adds: 'These facts and more about the geography of the North are to be found in the beginning of the *Gestae Arthuri*.'

Dee, commenting on this, writes that the book was 'a rare testimony of great importance to the British title to the *Septentrional* Regions, [and] Atlantis in particular'. Here, Atlantis actually means America, the land beyond the Atlantic, but the important word here is *Septentrional*, a word that refers not only to the region of the polar ice but also to the area of the heavens and the stars it contained, directly above it. We shall see why this is important in a moment.

Dee gives us a transcript of Mercator's translation ('word for word', he says) of Cnoyen's account, which was in turn based on the *Gestae Arthuri*, making a lineage that looks like this:

Gestae Arthuri [now lost]
Jacobus Cnoyen [now lost]
Principal Navigations by Mercator
Dee's version

Something of a palimpsest perhaps, and really coming down to our taking Mercator's word for it, or possibly Cnoyen's word for it. Here is most of Dee's version, slightly edited for sense:

In northern Norway ... where the sun never rises above the horizon there is sometimes a kind of dawn ... The passage there is difficult due of the seas which flow swiftly past Greenland ... This part of Northern Norway stretch to the mountains which surround the North Pole in a circle. It is also said that these mountains had amongst them certain cities, such as we find mentioned in the *Arthuri Gestis,* and there it is said dwell a race of small people ... All this and more concerning the northern regions are present at the beginning of the *Arthuri Gestis.* There we learn that in ancient times the Northern islands were called the *Ciliae,* now known as the *Septentrionals* ... and here were many small rivers which are called Indrawing Seas because the North pulls them with a great constant force ... Here there are great mountains reaching to the clouds, and the air is often clouded and dark ... *One group of Arthur's knights sailed thus far when he was conquering the Northern Isles and making them all subject to him.* [italics ours]

In the writings of the ancients it is said these Indrawing seas snatched some 4000 of Arthur's men, but that in 1364, eight descendants of these men visited the King of Norway ... One noble man, who had been a follower of Arthur, had, in the year 530, spent the winter in the northern half of Scotland, and one of his fleet had sailed to Iceland on the 3rd of May that year. At this time four ships returned from the North, and their captains warned Arthur about the strong currents. Because of this Arthur did not go any further, but nevertheless settled his people on the islands between Scotland and Greenland, and in Greenland itself.

There were some sailors on the four ships that returned who asserted that there were *magnetic rocks* under the water, and that eight of their fleet sank because of the iron nails with which they were constructed. After this Arthur fitted out a second fleet of 12 ships, made without iron, and sent forth 1800 men and 400 women. These set sail for the North on 5 May in the year after the earlier ships and set out. [At a guess 522. Ed.] Of these, five were driven onto rocks, but the rest survived and landed on the 18th of June on the 44th day after they had weighed anchor. (Trans J. Matthews)

Five from the twelve ships leaves seven and that, as we will see, is an important number.

Here is Arthur sending an expedition not only through the lands of Norway, Greenland and Iceland, but right to the North Pole itself, where, apparently, a number of cities are established. Dee was not certain whether these were founded by Arthur himself or were already there. However, there is a possible explanation for this, which will lead us even further north into the mysterious starry regions of the *Septentrionals*.

Dee mentions another text, the *Inventio Fortunata*, which he says was given to Edward III. Unfortunately this was among the volumes which vanished from Dee's library following his death, but we do know a little about its possible author and his curious (and possibly fictitious) voyage. The book is believed to have been written by Nicholas of Lynne, a Franciscan friar, mathematician and astronomer who attended Merton College in Oxford and was alive sometime around 1360. The earliest mention of his work is on the map drawn by Johannes Ruysch in 1508, where a high magnetic rock under the Arctic Pole is described. This may in fact be a mountain in the vicinity of Thule in Greenland well known to the medieval Icelanders, who had by the fourteenth century noticed the deviation of the compass the further north they travelled. Hakluyt believes this friar wrote the *Inventio Fortunata* after a voyage he made in 1360. Travelling in company with others to the northernmost islands of the world, he is said to have left his fellows and travelled on alone. The record of his travels, the *Inventio*, he presented to Edward III of England. This same friar 'for sundry purposes after that did five times pass from England thither, and home again'.[12]

Dee himself was convinced that this friar was another Minorite, Hugo of Ireland, a traveller who flourished and wrote *c.* 1360. It is only in recent years, however, that Nicholas of Lynne has acquired a considerable reputation as an early English explorer of the Arctic, in spite of the somewhat unlikely statement that he travelled alone to the Pole and later made five further arctic expeditions. However, the *Inventio Fortunata* was, as far as we can tell, a trustworthy description of Greenland and the Canadian archipelago, as far as these lands had been traversed by the medieval Icelanders of Greenland. Moreover, the book had a large circulation in Europe and may have been used by Columbus. Its author, whether Nicholas of Lynne or not, almost unquestionably received his information not firsthand by travelling through the Arctic but from a priest named Ivar Bárdarson, who travelled widely and acquired – directly or indirectly – much information about the eastern Canadian Arctic. Bárdarson was back in Norway between *c.* 1361 and 1364, and there the Oxford friar may have met him personally and compiled the *Inventio Fortunate* from his accounts. In any case, the excerpts from the *Inventio* found in later works point conclusively to an Icelandic-Greenlandic source.

This is all fascinating enough, but if we look just a little deeper behind the mythmaking of Dee's expansionist dreams, we find something even more fascinating lurking there. Dee mentions the '*Septentrional* regions' more than once in his work, referring both to a region of the North Polar ice and the pattern of stars above it. These stars include a constellation that is of particular importance: Boötes, one of a group that circle the pole star, and which includes the star Arcturus. This star, which is one of the brightest in the heavens, was considered so important at the time that the whole constellation was regularly called by its name.

The classical myth of Arcturus (see chapter 7) concerns the nymph Kallisto, who is raped by Zeus and eventually gives birth to Arkas. The goddess Hera, always jealous of Zeus' conquests, turns Kallisto into a bear. Years later, in one of those wonderful Freudian turns, Arkas, now king of Arcadia, unknowingly hunts down and almost kills his own mother before Zeus intervenes at the last moment and places them in the heavens together. Kallisto becomes the constellation

Ursa Major (The Great Bear) or *Arktos* in Greek. Arkas is the brilliant star *Arktouros*, which in Latin becomes Arcturus – the 'Bear Guardian' who is set to watch over his mother.

Given these names and the association with bears, it is perhaps not surprising that Arcturus has been associated with King Arthur for a long time. As so often in these stories it begins with the name. As we have seen, the star Arcturus was regularly used to describe the whole of the constellation of Boötes, and from at least the eleventh century onwards it was variously spelled Arturus, Arthurus, Artur and, once, even Arthur. Of course, this is at a time when there were no rules for spelling, and names in particular changed dramatically from text to text, but what is even more interesting here is the fact that this also happened in reverse – the name Arthur is regularly spelled Arcturus in a number of medieval manuscripts.

All of this may originate in the Latin interpretation of the Greek words for bear ('*arth*') and guardian ('*uthar*') – the understood meanings of the star names. *Uthar* is, of course, not too far from the name Uther, a name associated with Arthur's father from the earliest records.

Arth can also be translated as Bear-Man – or, according to one writer, as Arth-uthyr (pronounced Arth-Uir or Arth-ur), meaning Great or Wondrous Bear.

The connection of the name Arthur with the North Pole may go back even further. It is entirely possible that it stems from the name of the region itself – Arctic. This comes from the Latin *ar(c)ticus*, which in turn comes from the Greek *arktikos* meaning either 'of the Bear' or sometimes, more simply, 'northern'.

The Arctic was perceived as not only the northernmost part of the Earth but also a wholly mysterious place which became, for northern peoples especially, associated with the Land of the Dead. In the late twelfth and early thirteenth century, Arthur himself was known as *Ursus Horabulus*, 'the terrible bear', which is often thought to be applied to him because he raided religious properties to fund his warlike activities. In fact, it probably refers back to the starry associations of Arthur with Arcturus, since the rising and setting of the constellation was associated with savage and tempestuous weather.

We know that Arthur was associated with a great bear as far back as the tenth century. We find the constellation listed in the writings of Isidore of Seville and John of Sacrobosco, under various spellings, mostly with the letter 'c' dropped so that we end up with the same spellings: Arthurus, Arturus and Arthus. All these spellings were applied to Arthur at various times in the medieval period.

Given Arthur's status as a mythical or proto-historic king of increasing importance, it's not surprising if the connection grew with the telling. Only a mythic hero as important as Arthur could be named after a star!

There is still one further level of interpretation, of which Dee may or may not have been aware. Arthur's presence in the heavens is something that has been recognised for a long time. The Celts called the circuit described in the heavens by the constellation Ursa Major 'Arthur's Round Table', and in Welsh Ursa Major is still called *Arad'r Arthyr* – 'Arthur's Plough'. The stars of the constellation which we call the Plough are 'Arthur's Heifers' or 'Arthur's Wain' (Wagon), and Lyra is known as *Telyn Arthyr*, 'Arthur's Harp'.[13]

The description of Arthur's northern journey in Dee's researches has a ring of magic and myth about it. And it is curiously familiar. Where might we have heard of a voyage undertaken by Arthur, though wild waters to a strange and frozen land? We need look no further than the ninth-century poem *Prieddeu Annwfn*, attributed to the great poet and seer Taliesin. We think that at least one of the sources for this poem is from a distant memory of Arthur sailing off towards the far north. If so, it pushes the story of that voyage even further back in time. *Prieddeu Annwfn* was copied down in the ninth century but has been shown to date as far as 300 years earlier – to the sixth century, when one of the candidates for the real Arthur is believed to have lived.

The poem describes a voyage undertaken by Arthur and his heroes in search of a sacred vessel. This may well make it the oldest Grail story, which is also of interest here. For now, we just want to concentrate on two verses:

> Is not my song fit recital for kings,
> In the four-square Caer, in the Island of the Strong Door,
> Where noon and night make half-light,
> Where bright wine is brought before the host?
> Three ship burdens of Prydwen took to sea:
> Except seven none returned from Caer Rigor.
>
> I sing not for those whose shield-arms droop,
> Who know not the day nor the hour nor the cause
> when the glorious Son of Light was born...
> They know not who is the brindled, harnessed ox
> With seven score links upon his collar.
> When we went with Arthur on difficult errand;
> Except seven none returned from Caer Fandwy.
> (Translated by C. Matthews)

If we set this beside Dee's findings about Arthur's northern voyage, something very like a fully fledged mythic story emerges. This is complex stuff, and we are still unravelling its mysteries, but there are some clues.

Caer Rigor, one of seven cities mentioned in the poem, can be read to mean 'the Frozen Castle', which to us suggests Arthur was heading for the Arctic region. On the way he encounters a whirlpool that nearly sucks his ship under, though his ship manages to escape. This has been suggested as the Corry Vrecken, which lies off the west coast of Scotland at a place where waters rush between several islands, forming a whirlpool. Could this be another reference to the 'Indrawing Seas' mentioned by Dee and his sources and which apparently plagued Arthur's ships? Remember, out of the twelve ships he sent to the Arctic region only seven returned.

It's also interesting that Hell, for much of the Middle Ages, was described not as a place of heat and fire but of cold and ice. Surely this points directly to the frozen Arctic region, an icy Hell indeed and a version of the very Underworld to which Arthur sails! Even the half-light mentioned in the poem seems to refer to the dim light found in the Arctic regions for the greater part of the year.

Let's remember Dee's translation of the account from the *Gestae Arthuri*: '[T]here are mountains [around the North Pole] of which it is written that there were among them certain cities...'

There is an implication, as we saw, that Arthur himself may have founded the cities; or that he conquered them. So are the caers in the poem the cities of the Northern Polar Circle? Remember that this is a *mythic* interpretation not a geographic one, though the two may well come together in this account. If there is even a remote possibility of such an interpretation this leads to an interesting scenario.

Arthur sails with his men to the Far North, conquering everything in his path. He reaches the polar ice, where he either builds a series of cities or finds them already there and conquers them. There, perhaps, he learns of an ancient king who was once a hunter, and who bears a very similar name – Arktos. The memory of this mythic voyage is remembered in the poem by Taliesin and then expanded upon by later writers – beginning with Geoffrey of Monmouth, who had heard that Arthur made many northern conquests. Subsequent chroniclers followed this, and the now lost *Gestae Arthuri*, possibly describing a more detailed version of the story and listing all of Arthur's conquests in the north, added to Dee's idea of Arthur in the north. Elizabethan explorers such as Cnoyen, Hakluyt and others discovered this book and drew their own conclusions, including Arthur's northern kingdoms on their maps. Dee found these and made them part of his 'proof' that not only had Arthur existed but that Elizabeth was descended from him and inherited the right to rule not only over the whole of England but also over much of Scandinavia!

Then there is that enigmatic reference in the *Prieddeu Annwfn* to the mysterious beast with seven score starry links in his collar. Might not this refer to a constellation? Not Boötes unfortunately, as there are fewer than seven stars in the constellation, but this could be either a mistake or a misreading of an older source. Since there are references to the birth of a heroic child also in the *Prieddeu Annwfn* might it be stretching the point too far to suggest that all of this relates back an ancient cosmological myth in which Arthur is born among the stars?

Since there is a definite indication that the original form of Arthur's name was either Arktos or Arcturus, there is little doubt in our minds that the mythic Arthur was actually named after the star, which would certainly explain many of the attributes he later displayed in the myths.

It is also very interesting to note that whenever the version of Arthur's name is given the spelling of Arcturus it is *always* in connection with his mythic attributes, his departure for Avalon, his promise to return. No matter what other spellings are used this one is *always* applied to that otherworldly connection. And let us remember that stars rise and set in the heavens, vanishing during the day and reappearing at night, and of course that the stars also traversed the skies over the period of the year.

Arthur's undying nature and his connection with the stars was celebrated in John Lydgate's poem *The Fall of Princes* (*c.* 1430 CE), which may have been known to Dee. There, after the last battle of Camlann, in which Arthur is fatally wounded, like many heroes before him, he is taken up into the night sky, to the constellation of Boötes:

> Where he sits crowned in heavenly manner
> Amid the palace of stones crystalline
> Told among Christians first of the worthy nine.[14]

All of this points to the idea that behind John Dee's mythologising in the name of his queen there may lie a kernel of mythic truth, pointing to the real reason why he looked to the north in search of Arthur's furthest and most mysterious conquests. As such it relates precisely with the arguments we have produced regarding the importance of the Sword in the Stone motif and its connection with the Arthurian legends.

Appendix 2

CHRONOLOGY

Here is a rough chronology for the recording of tales concerning the Sword in the Stone:

c. 1250 BCE	Hittite (Sword in the Stone)
8th C BCE	Theseus (Sword under the Stone)
Late 3rd C BCE	Jason (no Sword)
5th C BCE	Herodotus (Sword in the Altar atop Wood)
Mid-1st C BCE–1st C CE	Mithras (Asia Minor and Rome, the Sword in the Bull)
Late 4th C CE	Alans (Sword in the Ground)
Mid-5th C	Attila (Sword on the Ground)
712–720	Japan (Sword in the Dragon's Tail)
c. 9th C	Finnian Cycle (Sword in the Ground)
Late 10th C	*Eddas* (Sword in the Tree)
c. 1180	Galgano (Sword in the Stone)

13th C	Robert de Boron (Sword in the Stone)
13th C	*Perlesvaus* (Crossbow Bolt in the Pillar)
c. 1200	Ogun (Sword in the Ground)
c. 1300–1320	*Lancelot* (Sword in the Grave)
c. 1470	Malory (Arthur; Sword in the Anvil atop the Stone; Lancelot, Sword on the Altar)
c. 1500	Ogun (voodoo) (Knife in the Ground)
1781	Felipe de Neve (Sword in the Stone via the Conquistadores)

NOTES

Preface

1. Matthews 1969, 1:15-20.
2. E.g., Jung and von Franz 1986, 163.
3. E.g., Stowe 1907.
4. Micha 1948-49:37-50; Littleton 1982:53-67; Malcor and Littleton 2000:181-194).
5. Barber and Barber 2004.
6. Barber and Barber 2004: 199. The world pillars are the constellations in which the sun rises at the solstices and equinoxes (Barber and Barber 2004:201).

Introduction

1. *Los Angeles Times*, April 27, 1931, p. A10.
2. 31.2.22; Hamilton 1986:414.
3. Littleton and Malcor 2000:26-39.
4. Micha and Morrisin Lacy et al. 1996.
5. Lacy 1986: 437-8.
6. Lacy et al. 1996.

7. Varner 2011: 16.

8. Varner 2011:67.

9. Varner 2011:67.

10. Barber and Barber 2004:211.

11. Puhvel 1987:22-23. See also Littleton 1970.

12. Puhvel 1987:23.

13. Puhvel 1987:24. See also Littleton 1970

14. Puhvel 1987:25. See also Littleton 1970.

15. Adapted from Barber and Barber 2004:210. The Barbers go on to say that Jesus Christ is associated with Gemini.

16. Recent scholarship suggests that the early Israelites were themselves Canaanites.

17. Somehow the 'Kingship in Heaven' also became scrambled with the tale of the Divine Twins in Germanic lore in a sequence that leads to Odin becoming the ruler of the gods.

18. Some scholars have suggested that this was part of the Egyptian attempt to recount the joining of Upper and Lower Egypt since the pattern keeps repeating.

19. Beckwith 2009: 30

20. Beckwith 2009: 36.

21. Beckwith 2009-30-57.

22. Beckwith 2009.

1 The Hittite Sword God

1. Gurney 1976:41. An earlier version of this chapter was presented by Linda A. Malcor on Friday, April 11, 2008, at the Annual Meeting of the Western States Folklore Society at the University of California, Davis. Another version was published in The Heroic Age 15 (October 2012) as 'The Hittite Sword in the Stone: The Sword god and his Twelve Companions' by Linda A. Malcor. See also Macqueen 1986, 28-29.

2. For a comprehensive overview of the hero tradition, sword-related and otherwise, see Miller 2000.

3. Gurney 1976:41.

4. Bryce 1998:360.

5. Zangger and Gautschy, 2019.

6. Bittel 1970:109; Gurney 1976:10; Zangger and Gautschy, 2019.

7. Teshub replaces Kumbari in the 'Kingship in Heaven' story (Macqueen 1986:149-150). For more on the 'Kingship in Heaven', see Littleton 1972.

8. Bittel 1970:109; Gurney 1976:10.

9. Deighton 1982:21,25.

10. Deighton 1982:25.

11. As far as Hebat is concerned, the sun goddess's name is still unknown, despite the fact that she, rather than Tarhu, was probably the head of the pantheon.

12. Macqueen 1986:111.

13. Macqueen 1986:119.

14. Bittel 1970:108.

15. 35 Zangger, Krupp, Demirel, and Gautschy. 2021: 57–94..

16. Bittel 1970:109.

17. Malcor 2012.

18. Gütterbock 1964:72; 1965:198.

19. In Malory, there were thousands of Knights of the Round Table, though only 150 could sit at the table. Continental sources give the number of Arthur's knights as twelve.

20. Macqueen 1986:58.

21. Macqueen 1986::59-60.

22. Gütterbock 1964:72; 1965:198.

23. Macqueen 1986:59-60.

24. Macqueen 1986: 61

25. Deighton 1982: 1.

26. Deighton 1982: 21, 25.

27. The fact that the war god had bulls sacrificed to him may have led to the confusion between the war god and the Hurrian Teshub.

28. It is possible that a variant existed where the Divine Warrior stabbed the World Tree itself.

29. Barber and Barber 2004: 100.

30. Macqueen 1986: 129.

31. Bittel 1970:108 f.; 1975:53, 61 ff.; Otten (1961, 130 ff.) gives the number of banished gods as eight.

32. Macqueen 1986: 129.

33. E.G., Wiggerman 1999.

34. Bittel 1970:109; Güterbock, 1964:72, 1965: 198.

35. Note that the twelve runners with the swords are on the western wall, and 'west' is the traditional direction of the Otherworld, the Land of the Dead, in many Indo-European traditions.

36. Laroche (1973:XIX) ; (Xenophon, Anabasis, v.v. 1; Apollonius Rhodius, *Argonautica*, ii, 1002 ff.; cf. Drews 1976: 26-9; Planhol, 1963: 298-305).' (Muhly, et al. 1985:74) is steel, shared meaning 'suggested for Greek χάλυω (Laroche 1973:xix) (Muhly, et al. 1985:76). *Hapalki.*

37. Muhly, et al. 1975, 76.

38. Muhly, et al. 1985, 74.

39. Mujly, et al. 1985, 74.

40. Macqueen 1986, 18.

41. Macqueen 1986, 52.

2 *The Greek Sword beneath the Stone*

1. Sword under the stone in Plutarch (*Theseus* chaps. 3-4.)

2. Walker 1995:16.

3. Walker 1995:15. 'Classical Greek culture' was spawned by the colonial Ionians, who settled on the coast and islands of Asia Minor following the invasion of the Dorians (Puhvel 1987:128). Hans Herter argued that Theseus was a pan-Ionian hero (Walker 1995:9-10). 'Lapiths represent ancient Ionians ... legends ... recall the occupation of Thessaly by Ionians before the Dorians invaded Greece' (Walker 1995:9-10). Walker (1995:13-14), however, proposes a Theseus from northeast Attica (Walker 1995:14). Ares 'headquartered' in Thrace and Hesphaistos in Lemnos 'where a pre-Greek population lingered in classical times' (Puhvel 1987:133). Herakles was another figure who predated the arrival of tales of Theseus.

4. Walker 1995:85. Poseidon may have originally gained his stronghold in the Peloponeseus 'during the second millennium' BCE (Puhvel 1987:132).

5. Walker (1996:86, 96) argues that Theseus originated from the Cretan Sea, but the evidence in the tale suggests that it simply traveled there from somewhere else, possibly becoming entangled with the Cretan Zeus material because of the Bear's Son element of the narrative before the story fractured into the two forms that appear in later Greek texts.

6. Kallisto may be splintered off from Artemis Kallistē ('Fairest Artemis'), and both 'Artemis and Arkas ... are dialectal cognates of [the Greek] árktos, 'bear'' (Puhvel 1987:136).

7. Allen 1963:92.

8. Hesiod (*c.* 700 BCE) called the star Arctouros ('Bear-guard') and Arctophilaxe ('Bear-watcher') (Allen 1963:93). Arkas was believed to be the celestial Arcturus, although writers as early as Ovid (43 BCE – 17 CE) scrambled Arcturus with Ursa Minor (Allen 1963:94), or even with Ursa Major (Allen 1963:98), sometimes in the same work.

9. Littleton presented parts of this chapter in a paper at the Western States Folklore Society meeting, April 20, 2007, at the University of California, Los Angeles.

10. Argonautica Book I. Trans. R.C. Seaton. Heinemann, 1967 p 3

11. Herodotus thought that Agenor predated his visit to Tyre ca. 450 BCE by 1,000 to 1,500 years. Herodotus. De Sélincourt 1954: 155.

12. In Greek myth these soldiers are human and considered to be the ancestors of the Thebans. In modern film, they are portrayed as undead skeletons, a serendipitous return to their likely origins.

13. Rose (1959: 264-266) cites the sword under the stone portion of the story to Apollodorus III, 206 foll. (*Apollodori Bibliotheca*, edited by Richard Wagner, Mythographi Graeci, Vol. 1, Lipsiae, Teubner, 1894); Plutarch, *Theseus*, 3 foll. Rose also equates Aigeus with Poseidon, following Farnell 1921: 86, 337. Rose notes (note 32, p. 282) that 'Theseus is probably a man, not a god.'

14. The editions of Apollodoros's *Bibliotheca* and Plutarch's *Life of Theseus* consulted in the chapter are, respectively, Hard 997 and Plutarch 974. See also Rose (1959, 264-266. Plutarch makes no mention of Theseus's putative divine parentage.

15. Perrin 1914: xi.

16. Perrin 1914: xi.

17. Perrin 1914: xi.

18. Perrin 1914: xiv.

19. Photius, *Bibliotheca*, p. 1452a, 37 sq., ed. Bekker.

20. Robert 1873; Frazer 1921, 1:ix.

21. Christ, p. 571; Frazer 1921, 1:xvi.

22. Robert 1873:34 sq.; cf. Frazer 1921, 1:xvii.

23. According to Rose (I1959, 264), the dual-parentage conundrum here may be resolved by the fact that Aigeus, the eponym of the Aegean Sea, is a localized form of Poseidon.

24. Ulansey 191.

25. Varner 2011: 50.

26. Varner 2011: 50.

27. Tripolitis 2002.

28. Plutarch. *'Life of Pompey'. Lives. 24 – via penelope.uchicago. edu.* – refers to events c. 68 BCE

29. Hinnells 1975, 2: 303-304.

30. Ulansey 1991: 29.

31. Puhvel 1987: 131-132.

32. Varner 2011: 16.

33. Varner 2011: 105.

34. Yaggy and Haines 1884; Varner 2011:109.

3 The Swords of Arthurian Tradition

1. Bryant 2001: 107-8.

2. Ibid. p108

3. Ibid. p109

4. Ibid. p110

5. Matthews 2000:9.

6. Davies 2018.

7. Benham 1902: 6.

8. Benham 1902: 12.

9. Matthews 2000:11

10. Loomis and Loomis 1938: 95.

11. B.N. Fr. 95, f. 159v. frontispiece; Loomis and Loomis 1938: 95, Fig.235.

12. Loomis and Loomis 1938: 95.

13. Matthews: 200: Chapter 2.

14. Bryant 2015.
15. B.N. Fr. 99 f. 561. Loomis and Loomis 1938: fig. 292, top register, right side.
16. Loomis and Loomis p. 109
17. Crozant, Dep Creuse. Loomis and Loomis p 109.
18. Loomis and Loomis p. 109.
19. B.N. Lat. 4915, f., 46 v. See Blum and Laurer, Miniature franç., XV-XVI century, pl. 13; Loomis and Loomis 1938: 109.
20. Matthews 2000: 193.
21. Loomis and Loomis, p. 99.
22. See Fig. 3, Loomis and Loomis, p. 99, fig. 253.
23. Littleton and Malcor: 2000: 26-8.
24. Webster 1951: 89.
25. Chrétien II. 1836-1996; Kibler 1981, pp. 79-85; cf. Lacy 1993: 80.
26. Lacy 1993:103
27. Bryant 1978.
28. Mason 1990'128.
29. Mason 1990:121.
30. Tony Tucker Author of *Sword Rests of the City*, published for the Friends of the City Churches https://www.london-city-churches.org.uk/cityevents/FCC_CE_2016.pdf

4 *Galgano's Embedded Sword*

1. Albergo and Pistolesi 1998:1.
2. Arbesmann 1961:16.
3. Garlaschelli thinks that the arms may have been found in 1694 and that they probably belonged to an individual who had been buried outside the chapel. If the story existed first, though, it's strange that a random find by late-17th century excavators would date to the correct century or that arms

alone would survive. They may simply have removed the arms and reburied the rest of the poor soul's remains where they found them.

4. Some sources give the year of Galgano's death as 1183, but 1181 seems to be the most commonly agreed-upon date ('San Galgano Or True Story, Legendary Sword,' http://www. italiantourism.com/news03.html).

5. The bishops who supposedly attended Galgano's funeral were from 'Volterra, Massa Marittima and Siena' (Albergo 1998:2). The 'Cistercian abbots of Fossanova' were also reportedly in attendance (Albergo 1998:2). Volterra erected in the fifth century; archdiocese of Pisa. Massa Marittima erected in the fifth century, archdiocese of Siena. Siena erected in the fourth century, elevated to Archdiocese 4/23/1459.

6. Arbesmann 1961:13.

7. Lugrianum; Arbesmann 1961:14.

8. Arbesmann 1961:15.

9. There may be a fifteenth-century transcript.

10. Arbesmann 1961:25.

11. *The Vita Merlini*. Ed and Trans Clarke.

12. Ross and Robins, 1989. *The Life and Death of a Druid Prince*; Miranda Aldhouse-Green and Val McDermid, 2015. *Bog Bodies Uncovered: Solving Europe's Ancient Mystery*.

13. John Matthews and Maarten Haverkamp, 2024.

14. Garlaschelli (personal communication) notes that georadar reveals sand and gravel under the chapel floor, and the rock of the hill lies beneath the gravel. 'What cannot be seen and is not sure, is if the stone having the sword is part of the same rock, (thus being the very tip of the hill, emerging just there), or if it is not, and could have been simply put there later.'

15. This may mean that the sword was not made locally or that something in the iron production process resulted in different amounts of trace metals in the sword and slag (Garlaschelli, personal communication).

16. Garlaschelli, pending publication.

17. Biologically, the skin shrinks as body fluids are lost, so hair and nails give the illusion of growing (Paul Barber, personal communication). This phenomenon is the source of many folk traditions all over the world.

18. Galgano's body is missing. The reliquary that contained his head is currently in Siena's Museo dell'Opera del Duomo (Phillips n.d.). The head is in the church of St. Michele in Chiusdino in a modern reliquary (Garlaschelli, personal communication)

19. Carroll 2001, The arms and hands may not have been on display until the eighteenth century or so (Luigi Garlaschelli, personal communication.)

20. Garlaschelli, personal communication.

21. Arbesmann 1961:10.

22. Arbesmann, 1961, MS C.VI.8 and MS G.I.2.

23. 'Galgano: in Bibliotheca Sanctorum (12 vols, Rome 1960-1970), Vol vi, p. 1.

24. Arbesmann 1961:5.

25. Arbesmann 1961:21-22, n. 43.

26. Arbesmann 1961:18. Later variants give three bishops as the entities fighting over the saint multiply.

27. Arbesmann 1961:27.

28. 'San Galgano Or True Story, Legendary Sword,' http://www.italiantourism.com/newso3.html).

29. Arbesmann 1961: 29-30.

30. Garlaschelli, unpublished article.

31. Without additional testing, there is no way to determine whose head might be in the reliquary.

32. Whatmough 1971: 208.

33. Whatmough 1971:209.

34. Grant 1980:81.

35. Whatmough 1971:213.

36. Whatmough 1971:213, 229.

37. Moiraghi 2003. Rory Carroll, 'Tuscany's Excalibur is the real thing, say scientists', Sunday, September 16, 2001, *The Observer*.

38. http://www.gypsyfire.com/Translation.htm

39. 'Sources,' 315. Jackson also takes Melconde to the form Melcon and then concludes that the name is a Norman corruption of the Old Welsh Mailcun, so the figure Galganu has been identified as the Middle Welsh Maelgwn.)

40. Cardini 2000:41.

41. Cardini 2000:42.

42. Arbesmann 1961:3.

43. http://www.municipio.re.it/IAT/iatRE.nsf/0/04B79C1A9ECA3207C1256CB40035D179?OpenDocument&lng=eng

44. Cardini 2000: 49.

45. Rose 1959:149

46. 1206, Innocent III, 'Galganus gilius Pancaldi, de maior progenie Vicecomitum' (Cfr. Vita scnati Galgani, p. 206); Benvnuti 2004:45.

47. It also appears in Euripides's Hec. 218 foll. See Allen, Hom. Op. V, p. 108.

48. Rose 1959:235.

49. Arbesmann 1961:19.

50. Technically, the range is 935-1035 CE because of the margin of error in thermoluminescence dating (Garlaschelli, personal communication).

51. Gorni 1999; Haynes 2000:5.

52. Arbesmann 1961:4.

53. If the chapel was originally something else, then Galgano's sarcophagus could have been buried there at a later date (Garlaschelli, personal communication).

54. 1181 also saw the death of Pope Alexander III (at Siena, Italy as Rolandus Bandinelli), so the 1183 date for Galgano's death proposed by some texts is impossible (Arbesmann 1961:25).

55. http://www.personal.psu.edu/users/w/x/wxk116/RomanCalendar/dec06.htm

56. The Hittite sword god, whose human body became a sword that slid into a fissure in a stone, is accompanied by an image of twelve marching/dancing soldiers and he may have been the Hittite god of the dead, a detail that equates well with the Roman Lupercus's tales of traversing the sky each day to collect the souls of the dead.

57. Arbesmann 1961:18

58. Arbesmann 1961:20.

59. Arbesmann 1961:21.

60. Garlaschelli, personal communication.

61. Cf. Bächtold-Stäubli 1987, 9:30]; Barber and Barber 2004: 167, n. 4.

5 The Scythians and the Sword in the Altar

1. 4.59-62; de Sélincourt 1972:290-291

2. Herodotus, Book 4, Sections 60-65

3. Yablonsky in Davis-Kimball, Bashilov and Yablonsky 1995:241.

4. Yablonsky 1995:249.

5. Cernenko 1983:15.
6. Cernenko 1983:15.
7. Cernenko 1983: 16.
8. Cernenko 1983:17.
9. Sulimirski 1970:36, de Sélincourt 1972:290.
10. Sykes 1915:411
11. Geographic Journal,1907
12. Ammianus Marcellinus 2.18.
13. Ammianus Marcellinus 31.4.22; Rolfe 1936:3 95; Littleton 1982; Littleton and Malcor 2000: xxvvii, 186.
14. Herodotus 4.59-62; de Sélincourt 1972:290-291.
15. Puhvel 1987:133.
16. Puhvel 1987:133.
17. Ammianus Marcellinus. *The Late Roman Empire* Book 31 ch.4
18. Varner 2011: 21.
19. W.S. Allen 1965: 159-172; John Colarusso 2002: 192-196.
20. Probably the three brothers who received the three golden objects from the sky, exactly backward from the Christian forging swords into plowshares.
21. Colarusso 2002:241.
22. 'Saga 86: The Birth of Sosruquo'; Colarusso 2002:388.
23. Colarusso 2002:395.
24. Colarusso 2002:216-218.
25. Colarusso 2002:218.
26. Saga 89, Colarusso 2002:401-404.
27. Colarusso 2002:402.
28. Colarusso 2002:404.

6 The West African Sword in the Earth

1. Burton, Richard Francis 'Abeokuto and the Camaroons Mountains, p. 229)

2. Lawson 1985:50. An earlier version of this chapter was presented by the authors at the 2004 Annual Meeting of the California Folklore Society, Northridge, CA. We have regularized the spelling to 'Ogun' throughout in order to avoid confusion. There are many variants of the spelling of this deity's name, e.g. Oggún (González-Wippler 1975:15).

3. Littleton and Malcor 2000:181-194.

4. Barnes 1989:2; Lawson 1985:61; Drewal in Barnes 1989:227. In Íjálá chants, Ogun is associated with rainwater as well as the hunt and the king (Babalola in Barnes 1989:160). Ogun is also a god of safety in travel (Lawson 1985:62). He is 'of the great family of Nago loa' (Métraux 1959:107).

5. Barnes 1989:1.

6. FAMA 1993:228.

7. Lawson 1985:62.

8. Barnes 1989:53; Mercier 1954:233; Lawson 1985:61

9. Barnes, Sandra (1997). *Africa's Ogun: Old World and New.* Bloomington Ind: Indiana University Press.

10. Brown in Barnes 1989:78; Brown 1980:28.

11. Lawson 1985:61; Brown in Barnes 989:78; Pemberton 1977:20.

12. Métraux 1959:80, 166.

13. Herodotus 4.62; 1972:290.

14. Barnes and Ben-Amos in Barnes 1989:58.

15. E.g., Dumezil 1958, Littleton 1982; Puhvel 1989:159-160.

16. Métraux 1959:92, 109-110, 167; Babalola in Barnes 1989:165; Forbes 1966: 236, 242.

17. Drewal in Barnes 1989:239.

18. Drewal in Barnes 1989:241.

19. The thunder connection seems to arise from the sound of battles (Métraux 1959:107).

20. Forbes 1966:120.

21. Davis-Kimball 2002:65-66, 121.
22. Traditional Festivals, Vol. 2 [M-Z] ABC-CLIO 2005, p. 346.
23. Métraux 1959:145.
24. Pemberton in Barnes 1989:130; Idowu 1962:86.
25. Ackerman 1952:59.
26. Sulimirski 1970:36.
27. von Sydow 1965:231-232.
28. Gurdasani, Deepti; et a;/ 'The African Genome Variation Project Shapes Medical Genetics in Africa.' Nature 517 (7534): 327-332
29. Shaw 1978:82.
30. Barnes 1989:53; Williams 1973:148-52.
31. Barnes 1989:6.
32. Armstrong in Barnes 1989:30.
33. Bennett 1975:24.
34. Fage 1978:53.
35. Abimbola 2005..
36. 'Oduduwa, The Ancestor of the Crowned Yoruba Kings'.
37. Yoruba in Ghana – The Nigerian Journal of Economic and Social.
38. Falola and Childs 2005.
39. Domingues da Silvam Sanile B.; Misevich 2018.
40. Métraux 1959:126; Drewal in Barnes 1989:211; cf. Barnes 1989:14.
41. Métraux 1959:161; see also 325.
42. Senior 2005.
43. Brown in Barnes 1989:78.
44. Brown in Barnes 1989: 88, note 10.
45. Métraux 1959:112
46. The names Erinlà and Ogun are both ancient, though no suitable etymological origin has been offered for either of them (Babalola in Barnes 1989:169, note 4).

47. Babalola in Barnes 1989:169, note 2. Hinnells 1975, vol. 2, pp. 303-304.
48. Brown in Barnes 1989:78.
49. Dorsey 2020.
50. Drewal in Barnes 1989:223.
51. Drewal in Barnes 1989:227; cf. Bachrach 1973:21-22)
52. Barnes 1980; Barnes 1989:4.
53. Barnes 1989:4-5; Lévi-Strauss 1966:16-22; Armstrong in Barnes 1989:5.
54. Shaw 1978:84.
55. Shaw 1978:84.
56. Shaw 1978:85; Davies 1966:471; Davies 1973; Diop 1968; Coghlan 1941; Lambert 1971, 1973.
57. Shaw 1978:85.
58. Barnes and Ben-Amos in Barnes 1989:42; see also van der Merwe 1980:464.
59. Barnes 1989:42; see also Calvocoressi and David 1979:10-11). The process was 'well established' in Benin 'by the thirteenth to fourteenth centuries' (Barnes 1989:42).
60. Métraux 1959:95. 109.
61. Métraux 1959:95. 109.
62. Armstrong in Barnes 1989:32, 34.
63. Dumézil 1978:24-25; see also Dumézil 1930: 52.
64. Pemberton in Barnes 1989:139, note 3.
65. Armstrong in Barnes 1989:34.
66. Barnes 1989:34.
67. Shaw 1978:86.
68. Shaw 1978:85; Green 1975:20.
69. Shaw 1978:70; Connah 1967:24; Connah 1968:317.
70. Shaw 1978:86.
71. Shaw 1978:86; Mauny 1947; Lhote 1966.

72. Herodotus, 4.181-188; de Sélincourt 1972:332-333; Shaw 1978:86. It is possible that Hanno of Carthage took a sea route ca. 470 B.C. to the west coast of Africa near the region that became Nigeria.

7 *The Germanic, Icelandic and Irish Swords*

1. E.g., Bruce 1958, 1:145..
2. Puhvel 1987:189.
3. Puhvel 189-190. There is a little information from 'Frankish and Langobard laws' and from Anglo-Saxon literature, but none of these contain the story of the Sword in the Branstock (Puhvel 1987:190).
4. Puhvel 1987:190.
5. Puhvel 1987:190.
6. Bonwick 1894.
7. *Ancient Laws of Ireland: Din tectugad and certain other selected Brehon Law tracts.* H.M. Stationery Office. 1879.
8. Borlase 1887: 883.
9. Borlase 1887: 884-5.
10. Borlase 1887: 884-5.
11. Littleton and Malcor 1985: 161-182.
12. Borlase 1887: 885.
13. Borlase 1887: 886.
14. Borlase 1887: 887.
15. Lincoln 1981: 87 ff.
16. Windisch Lines 4009-16.
17. Windisch and Dunn, Lines 4732 ff.
18. Sayers 2013: 1–18.
19. Spenser 1763.
20. Henderson 1966.
21. Guerber 1985: 253-258.

22. Puhvel 1987:202.

23. Poetic Edda, Hāvamāl 138; Puhvel 1987: 194.

24. Puhvel 1987:218.

25. Puhvel 1987: 218.

26. Wells 2001:120.

27. Wells 2001:121.

28. Wells 2001:116.

29. Wells 2001: 115-117.

30. Wells 2001: 115-117.

31. Bruce 1958:145.

32. *Gallic War* 8.10 1901: 230-231.

33. Wells 2001:121.

34. Millar 1966:276.

35. Millar 1966:115.

36. Millar 1966: 115. The Nuristae may be the same people that Herodotus calls the 'Neuri'.

37. Millar 1966:284.

38. Millar 1966:289

39. Todd 1992:24.

40. Millar 1966:289.

41. *Germania* 46; Mattingly and Handford 1970:140. These were the Peucini (Bastarnae), Venedi and Fenni.

42. Owen 1985: 28-29; Varner 2011: 104.

43. Guerber 2006: 96; Varner 2011: 106.

44. Varner 211: 105.

45. Ward 1981, 2:16, no. 381.

46. Jordanes 35.183; Mierow 1915:102-103. Ward says 'Cf. *Altdeutsche Wälder*, I, 212, Note 10 and p. 319. Cr. Also *Lamb. Schafnab.*, p. 348:

47. Mills 1933: 60 ff. Attila also figures in the Icelandic *Saga of Hrolf Kraki*, albeit as an opponent of rather than a wielder of the sword.

48. Mills 1933:45.

49. Mills 1933:49.

50. Varner 2011: 66/

51. Milisauskas 1978:253.

52. Milisauskas 1978:254; Phillips 1980:228.

53. Hedeager 1992:13.

54. Varner 2011: 68.

55. Davidson 1988: 216.

56. Varner 2011: 81.

57. Sturluson 1987: 101.

58. Varner 2011: 84.

8 *The Japanese Sword*

1. The most consistent and straight-forward account of this and other aspects of Japanese mythology is contained in the *Kojiki*, which appears to be based on wholly indigenous sources. The *Nihonshioki*, although complied less than a decade after Ono Susumu completed the *Kojiki*, draws on a variety of slightly different texts (e.g., there are multiple versions of almost every story) and is far more influenced by ancient Chinese mythology (see Philippi 1968:15-18). We rely primarily on the *Kojiki* versions of the events in question. The linear citations come from the English translations, respectively, by Donald Philippi and W. G. Aston and are not present in the original texts.

2. *Kojiki* 1.14-17; *Nihonshoki* I.29-30.

3. *Kojiki* 1.17; *Nihonshoki* I.37-41.

4. *Kojiki* 1.19; *Nihonshoki* 1.51.

5. The creature is also sometimes called Koshi Yamata no Orochi, after a region in Southwest Honshu in what is now Shimane Prefecture.

6. *Kojiki* 1.19.20; *Nihonshoki* 1:51-52.

7. *Kojiki* 1.19.21.

8. Barber and Barber 2005:240; Blust 2000; Newman 1979:110-115.

9. *Kojiki* 1.19.8

10. Littleton 1981:273-274.

11. *Kojiki* 1.38-39; *Nihonshoki* II.1-3.

12. A sacred replica of the sword, together with replicas of the other two divine objects, is still presented to each new Japanese emperor at his enthronement.

13. *Kojiki* 2.47-52; *Nihonshoki* III.

14. *Kojiki* 2.77-88; *Nihonshoki* VII.18-40; see also Littleton 1995.

15. *Kojiki* 2.80.1-16; *Nihonshoki* VII.18-19.

16. In a way, this episode recalls Susanō's getting Yamata no Orochi drunk before killing him, and, as we shall soon see, it was shortly afterward that Yamato-takeru gained possession of the wondrous sword.

17. *Kojiki* 2.80.15; *Nihonshoki* VII.19.

18. As late as the end of the twelfth century CE there appears to have been a significant number of Ainu in this region. Indeed, in 1185, the first Shōgun, Yoritomo (Hall 1970:87), was given the formal title 'Generalissimo [Shogun] in Charge of the Eastern Barbarians [the Emeshi, or Ainu].' Ironically, this title lasted until 1867, centuries after the Ainu had totally disappeared from the Island of Honshu, let alone the Kanto region.

19. *Kojiki* 2.82.6; *Nihonshoki* VII.23.

20. *Kojiki* 2.83; *Nihonshoki* VII.23.

21. *Kojiki* 2:85; *Nihonshoki* VII.29.

22. *Kojiki* 2.86; *Nihonshoki* VII.29.

23. Littleton 2008.

24. Varner 2011: 70.

25. E.g., Dumézil 1930:61-63.

26. Littleton and Malcor 2000: 181ff, 154ff.
27. For the parallels between the death scenes of Arthur and Batraz, please see Grisward 1969 and Littleton and Malcor 2000: xxv-xxvi, 66-71.
28. Dumézil 1930:69.
29. *Kojiki* 2:88; *Nihonshoki* VII.31.
30. Varner 2011: 89.
31. Mair 1983:141.
32. Namio Egami 1964, 1967.
33. Ledyard 1975; Yoshida 1962, 1974, 1977.
34. Littleton 1995:263.
35. Cf. Littleton 1982:10.
36. Yoshida 1979; see also Obayashi and Yoshida 1981.
37. For an in-depth discussion and assessment of Dumézil's tripartite model, see Littleton 1982.
38. Littleton 1995:263; Vernadsky 1943:82-84.
39. Maenchen-Helfen 1973:280.
40. Kao 1960.
41. Maenchen-Helfen 1973:280.
42. Varner 2011: 18-19.
43. Varner 2011: 21.
44. Dumézil 1930:54; Littleton 1995:271.
45. Obayashi 1975.

9 Zodiacal Lore and Legend

1. Krupp 1978: 262-263.
2. Barber and Barber 2004:198, fig. 35.
3. Barber and Barber 2004: 199.
4. Based on Barber and Barber 2004:209-210.
5. For the purposes of this discussion, we will only be talking about the night sky as viewed from the Northern

Hemisphere, so the Pole Star we are concerned about is whatever is at the end of the celestial pole as it points north from above the equator.

6. Ursa Minor is adjacent to the constellation Draco.

7. Barber and Barber 2004:201.

8. Barber and Barber 2004:198-199.

9. Barber and Barber 2004:208, n. 15; for the Japanese variant, see Littleton 1981 and Chapter 8.

10. Barber and Barber 2004:198.

11. Based on Barber and Barber 2004: 211.

12. Barber and Barber 2004:198-199. The Egyptians oriented their pyramids so that the shaft through which the pharaoh's soul would travel to the pole star, Thuban. For the Japanese variant, see Littleton 1981.

13. Barber and Barber 2004:198.

14. Based on Barber and Barber 2004: 211.

15. Macqueen 1986, 29, 36. Influence from the steppes can be seen in the weaponry depicted at Yazılıkaya.

16. Barber and Barber 2004: 208.

17. Even when there is no observable pole star, it is still possible to discern the position of the celestial pole, the imaginary extension of the earth's axis into space, by noting the positions of the various constellations.

18. Thompson 1946: 396ff. 430ff.

19. Thompson 1946: 13 ff., 176.

20. Thompson 1946: 442.

21. Barber and Barber 2004: 250.

22. Ulansey 1989.

23. Barber and Barber 2004:206.

24. Puhvel 1987:137.

25. Cf. Littleton 2007.

26. As we discuss in Chapter 1, offerings to the Hittite sword god were also made underground.
27. Hipparchos' calculation of the cycle was off by about 10,000 years (Barber and Barber 2004: 205).
28. The seven layers of earth that figure in some of the tales are the celestial spheres, through all of which the Divine Sword cuts.
29. Sullivan 1996, 80; Barber and Barber 2004:200.
30. Littleton and Malcor 2000: 181-193.
31. Ridpath, 1994, associates the Altar with the story of Centaurus sacrificing Lupus in Roman mythology.
32. Herodotus 4.59-62; de Sélincourt 1972:290-291.
33. Spenser 1763: 90-91.
34. Littleton and Malcor 2000: 18-26.
35. Egyptians/pyramids/Thuban.
36. Milisauskas 1978: 253.
37. Milisauskas 1978:254.
38. Shutz 1983:09.
39. Hedeager 1992:13.

Appendix 1: Arthur and the Voyage North

1. Decosta 1881.
2. We are indebted to the researches of Dr. Caitlin Green in the essay 'King Arthur, the Arctic and Arcturus' in *The Heroic Age: A Journal of Early Medieval Northwestern Europe*, 15 (October 2012), 2012. See Dee 2004; Artese, 33.1, 2003: 125-41.
3. https://www.aldvavall.com/admin/uploads/BOOKS_PDFs/John_Dee_-_General_and_Rare_Memorials_Pertaining_to_Perfecte_Arte_of_Navigation.pdf
4. Dee 2004.

5. Ibid.
6. Dee 1842; French 1972.
7. Dee 2004: 68.
8. Dee 2004: 38-9.
9. Giles and Bell 1910: 242-243.
10. Taylor 1956: 56-68.
11. Ibid p63
12. Dee 2004: 84
13. Anderson 2004: 240.
14. https://collections.library.yale.edu/catalog/16371223.

BIBLIOGRAPHY

Aarne, Antti. 1961. *Types of the Folktale*. Enlarged and translated by Stith Thompson. *FF Communications* 184. Helsinki: Suomalainen Tiedeakatemia Academia Scientiarum Fennica.

Abimbola, Kola. 2005. *Yoruba Culture: A Philosophical Account*. Iroko Academics.

Ackerman, Robert William. 1952. *An Index of the Arthurian Names in Middle English*. Stanford: Stanford University Press.

Agrawal, D. P. 2000. *Ancient Metal Technology and Archaeology of South Asia: a Pan-Asian Perspective*. New Delhi: Aryan Book International.

Ahmed, Sami Said. 1975. *The Yazidis: Their Life and Beliefs*. Henry Field, ed. Florida: Field Research Projects.

Albergo, Vito, and Andrea Pistolesi. 1998. *San Galgano*. English edition. Firenze: Centro Stampa Editoriale Bonechi.

Allen, N. J. 1987. 'The Ideology of the Indo-Europeans: Dumézil's Theory and the Idea of a Fourth Function.' *Journal of Moral and Social Studies* 2:23-39.

Allen, Richard Hinckley. 1963. *Star Names: Their Lore and Meaning*. New York: Dover.

Ammianus Marcellinus. 1939. *Ammianus Marcellinus*. J. C. Rolfe, trans. Cambridge, MA: Harvard University Press.

-----. 1982. *The Later Roman Empire*. Walter Hamilton, trans. New York: Penguin Classics.

-----. 1986. *The Late Roman Empire (AD 354-378)*. Walter Hamilton, trans. London: Penguin Books.

Anderson, Graham 2004. *King Arthur in Antiquity*. London & New York: Routledge.

Anderson, Graham, and Alfred P. Smyth. 2007. *The Earliest Arthurian Texts: Greek and Latin Sources of the Medieval Texts*. Ceredigion: Mellen.

Anonymous. 1879. *Ancient Laws of Ireland: Din tectugad and certain other selected Brehon Law tracts*. H.M. Stationery Office.

Arbesmann, Rudolph. 1961. 'The Three Earliest *Vitae* of St. Galganus.' In *Didascaliae: Studies in Honor of Anselm M. Albareda*. Sesto Prete, ed. New York: Bernard M. Rosenthal, pp. 1-37.

Artese, C. 2003. 'King Arthur in America: Making Space in History for *The Faerie Queene* and John Dee's *Brytanici Imperii Limites*.' In *Journal of Early Medieval and Modern Studies* 33(1):125-41.

Bachrach, Bernard S. 1973. *A History of the Alans in the West*. Minneapolis: University of Minnesota Press.

Bächtold-Stäubli, Hanns. 1927/1987. *Handwörterbuch des deutschen Aberglaubens*. Berlin: de Gruyter.

Bajpai, K. D. 1998. 'Iron Metallurgy in Ancient Madhya Pradesh.' In *Archaeometallurgy in India*. Vibha Tripathi, ed. Delhi: Sharada, pp. 274-277.

Bakhuizen, S. C. 1997. 'Greek Steel.' *World Archaeology* 9(2):220-234.

Barber, Elizabeth Wayland, and Paul T. Barber. 2004. *When They Severed Earth From Sky: How the Human Mind Shapes Myth* Princeton and Oxford: Princeton University Press.

Barker, Graeme, and Tom Rasmussen. 2000. *The Etruscans.* Massachusetts, Oxford and Australia: Blackwell.

Barnes, Sandra T. 1980. *Ogun: An Old God for a New Age.* ISHI Occasional Papers in Social Change, #3. Philadelphia: ISHI.

-----. ed. 1989. *Africa's Ogun.* Bloomington and Indianapolis: Indiana University Press.

Beckwith, Christopher I. 2009. *Empires of the Silk Road: A History of Eurasia from the Bronze Age to the Present.* Princeton, NJ: Princeton University Press.

Bennet, Norman R. 1975. *Africa and Europe.* New York: Holmes and Meier.

Benvnuti, Ann. 2004. *La spada nella roccia: San Galgano e l'epopea eremitica di Montesiepi.* Firenze: Mandragora.

Bittel, Kurt. 1970. *Hattusha, Capital of the Hittites.* New York: Oxford University Press.

-----. 1975. *Boğazköy-Hattuša. IX. Das hethitische lgheiligtum Yazılıkaya.* Berlin.

Bocoum, Hamady, ed. 2004. *The Origins of Iron Metallurgy in Africa: New Light on its Antiquity: West and Central Africa.* Paris: UNESCO.

Bogacki, P. Jan. 1997. *Saint Michael Shrine on the Gargano.* Edizioni del Santuario.

Bonwick, James. 1894. *Irish Druids and Old Irish Religions.* London: Sampson Low, Marston & Co., Ltd.

Brengle, Richard L., ed. 1964. *Arthur, King of Britain: History, Chronicle, Romance and Criticism, with Texts in Modern English from Gildas to Malory.* New Jersey: Prentice-Hall.

Brezinski, Richard, and Mariusz Mielczarek. 2002. *The Sarmatians 600 BC–AD 450.* Oxford: Osprey Publishing.

Brighenti, Francesco, compiler. 1998. 'Horses in Protohistoric India.' https://www.svabhinava.org/AITvsOIT/HorsesIndia-IndologyList-frame.php. Accessed 12/17/23.

Bruce, James Douglas. 1958. *The Evolution of Arthurian Romance from the Beginning Down to the Year 1300.* 2nd ed. Gloucester: Peter Smith. 2 vols.

Bryant, C. 2015. *Parliament: The Biography.* Vol. 1: *Ancestral Voices.* Transworld.

Bryant, N. Trans. 1978. *The High Book of the Grail: A translation of the 13th century Romance of Perlesvaus.* Cambridge. D. S. Brewer.

-----, trans. 2001. Robert de Boron, *Merlin and the Grail.* D. S. Brewer.

Bryce, Trevor. 1998. *The Kingdom of the Hittites.* Oxford: Oxford University Press.

Burton, Richard Francis. 1883. *The Book of the Sword.* Whitefish, MT: Kessinger Reprint. 1987. New York: Dover Publications, Inc.

Byock, Jesse L. 1998. *The Saga of King Hrolf Kraki.* London and New York: Penguin.

Caesar, Julius. 1901. *Eight Books of Caesar's Commentaries on the Gallic War Literally Translated With Explanatory Notes.* Excelsior Translations. New York: Platt and Nourse.

Calvocoressi, D., and N. David. 1979. 'A New Survey of Radiocarbon and Thermoluminescence Dates for West Africa.' *Journal of African History* 20:1-29.

Campbell, John Gregory. 2005. *The Gaelic Otherworld.* Edinburgh: Birlinn.

Cardini, Franco. 2000. *San Galgano e la spada nella roccia.* Siena: Cantagalli.

Carroll, Rory. 2001. 'Tuscany's Excalibur is the real thing, say scientists.' *The Observer*, Sunday, September 16.

Carlton, David and Richard J. Moll. 2018. 'The Arundel *Coronatio Arthuri*: A Middle English Sword in the Stone Story from London, College of arms MS, Arundel 58.' *Arthurian Literature* vol. XXXIV:89-130.

Chakrabarti, D. K. 1992. *The Early Use of Iron in India*. Madras: Oxford.

Charachidzé, Georges. 1986. *Prométhée ou le Caucase*. Paris: Flammarion.

Chickering, Howell D., Jr., trans. 1977. *Beowulf: A Dual-Language Edition*. New York: Anchor Books.

Christ, Wilhelm von. 1831-1906. *Geschichte der griechischen Litteratur*. https://archive.org/details/ geschichtedergri21chriuoft. Accessed 12/17/23.

Cinelli, F. 1993. 'Shedding Light on Etruscan Origins: Mitochondrial DNA Studies Launched.' In *Amici di Spannocchia Newsletter* 13:5. Harmondsworth and New York: Penguin. 2 vols.

Coghlan, H. H. 1941. 'Prehistoric Iron Prior to the Dispersal of the Hittite Empire.' *Man* 41:76-77.

Connah, Graham 1967. 'Progress Report on Archaeological Work in Bornu 1964-1966.' In *Northern History Research Scheme Second Interim Report*. Zaria, pp. 20-31.

-----. 1968. 'Radiocarbon Dates for Benin City and further Dates for Daima, N.E. Nigeria.' In *Journal of the Historical Society of Nigeria* 4(2):313-20.

-----. 1981. *Three Thousand Years in Africa*. Cambridge: Cambridge University Press.

Cooper, J. C. 1978. *An Illustrated Encyclopedia of Traditional Symbols*. London: Thames and Hudson.

Coppens, Philip. 2007. 'The Road Not Taken.' *Les Carnets Secrets* 7 http://www.philipcoppens.com/mithras.html. Accessed 12/12/23.

Crooke, William. 1894. 'Folktales of Hindustan.' *Indian Antiquary* 23:78-80.

Cumont, Franz. 1903. *The Mysteries of Mithra*. Chicago: The Open Court publishing company.

Dale, Sharon. 1997. 'To the Victors Goes the Hagiography: The Cistercian Frescoes at San Galgano and The Vitae Galgani.' *Citeaux* 48:231-59.

Davidson, Hilda R. Ellis. 1969. *Scandinavian Mythology*. London, New York, Sydney, and Toronto: Paul Hamlyn.

Davies, O. 1966. 'Comment on "The Iron Age in sub-Saharan Africa" by A.J. Arkell, Brian Fagan and Roger Summers.' *Current Anthropology* 7: 470-471.

-----. 1973. *Excavations at Ntereso, Gonja, Northern Ghana.* Final Report. Roneo'd.

Davies, Sioned. 2018. *The Mabinogion*. Oxford: Oxford University Press.

Davis-Kimball, Jeannine. 2003. *Warrior Women: An Archaeologist's Search for History's Hidden Heroines*. New York: Warner Books.

Decosta, B.F. 1881. *Myvyrian Archaeology: the pre-Columbian Voyages of the Welsh to America*. Albany: J. Munsell's Sons.

Dee, John. 2004. *The Limits of the British Empire*. Ed and trans K. MacMillan and J. Abeles. Westport: Praeger.

De la Tour, Henri. 1892. *Atlas de Monnaies Gauloises*. Paris: Library Plon.

De Michele, P. F. n.d. *Sur le Gargano apparut l'Archange: Guide touristique du Sanctuaire et de la ville de Monte Sant'Angelo*. Lily Faure, trans. Foggia Viale di Vittorio: Leone.

De Sélincourt, Aubrey, trans. 1954. Herodotus, *The Histories*. London and New York: Penguin.

Deighton, Hilary J. 1982. 'The "Weather-god" in Hittite Anatolia: An Examination of the Archaeological and Textual Sources.' *Biblical Archaeology Review*, International Series 143.

Dickson, Arthur. 1929. *Valentine and Orson: A Study in Late Medieval Romance*. New York: AMS.

Diop, L-M. 1968. 'Métallurgie traditionelle et âge du fer en Afrique.' *Bull. Inst. Fond. Afr. Noire*. B, 30:10-38.

Dorsey, Lilith. 2020. *Orishas, Goddesses, and Voodoo Queens: The Divine Feminine in the African Religious Traditions*. Weiser Books.

Dumézil, Georges. 1930. *Légendes sur les Nartes*. Paris: Librairie ancienne Honoré Champion.

-----. 1948. *Mitra-Varuna: Essai sur deux représentations indo-européenes de la souverineté*. Paris: Gallimard.

-----. 1958. *L'idéologie tripartite de Indo-Européens*. Brussels: Collection Latomus 25.

-----. 1972. *The Destiny of a King*. (Part 3 of *Mythe et epopee II*.) Alf Hiltebeitel, trans. Chicago: University of Chicago Press.

-----. 1978. *Romans de Scythie et alentour*. Paris: Payot.

Ernst, B. R. and T. J. E. de Vries. 1961. *Atlas of the Universe*. H. E. Butler, ed. D. R. Welsh, trans. Paris: Nelson.

Evola, Jacques (trans. G. Stucco). 1997. *The Mystery of the Grail: initiation and magic in the quest for the spirit*. Rochester, Vermont: Inner Traditions, pp. 31-32.

Fage, J. D. 1978. *A History of Africa*. New York: Alfred A. Knopf.

Fagg, B. E. B. 1969. 'Recent Work in West Africa: New Light on the Nok Culture.' In *World Archaeology* 1(1):41-50.

Falola, Toyin, and Mait D. Childs. 2005. *The Yoruba Diaspora in the Atlantic World (Blacks in the Diaspora)*. Bloomington, Indiana: Indiana University Press.

Farnell, Lewis Richard. 1921. 'Greek Hero-Cults and Ideas of Immortality.' *The Gifford Lectures delivered in the University of St. Andrews in the year 1920*. Oxford: Oxford University Press.

Fáróunbi Àìná Mosúnmọ lá Adéwálé-Somadhi, Chief. 1993. *Fundamentals of the Yorùbá Religion (Òrìsá Worship)*. San Berbardino, California: Ilé Òrúnmìlà Communications.

Faulkes, Anthony, ed. 1979. *Two Versions of Snorra Edda from the 17th Century*. 2 vols. Reykjavik, Iceland: Stofnun Árna Magnússonar Steinholt (CK).

Flueckiger, Joyce Burkhalter. 1996. *Gender and Genre in the Folklore of Middle India*. Ithaca and London: Cornell.

Forbes, Frederick E. 1966. *Dahomey and the Dahomans*, Volume 2. London: Frank Cass.

Fortson IV, Benjamin W. 2004. *Indo-European Language and Culture*. Massachusetts: Blackwell.

Frazer, James George. 1921. *Apollodorus, The Library*, 2 vols. Cambridge, Massachusetts and London: Harvard, Loeb Classical Library.

French, P. J. 1972. *John Dee: the World of an Elizabethan Magus*. London: Routledge.

Galetti, Torchj Dei Gius, and Noah Moerbeek. 2014. *The True Story of the Sword in the Stone: A compendium on the Life of St Galgano*. Sarah Grant, ed. Ryan Grant, trans. Post Falls, ID: Mediatrix Press.

Garlaschelli, Luigi. 2001. 'La Spada nella Roccia.' *Focus*.

-----. 2006. 'The *real* Sword in the Stone.' *Skeptical Inquirer* 30(3):40 ff.

Germanicus Caesar. 1976. *The Aratus ascribed to Germanicus Caesar.* D.B. Gain, ed. London: Athlone.

Giles, J. A. and G. Bell, eds. and trans. 1910. *Six English Chronicles.* London: George Bell.

Ginzel, E. A. 1995. 'Steel in Ancient Greece and Rome.' https:// dtrinkle.matse.illinois.edu/MatSE584/articles/steel_greece_ rome/steel_in_ancient_greece_an.html. Accessed 12/17/2023.

Gokhale, B. G. 1952. *Ancient India: History and Culture.* Bombay *et al.*: Asia.

Gonzaléz-Wippler, Migene. 1975. *Santeria: African Magic in Latin America.* New York: Anchor Books.

Gorni, Allesandro. 1999. 'Montesiepe.' http://www.ninogorni. com/original/graphics/drw2i.htm. Accessed 3/23/05.

Grant, Michael. 1980. *The Etruscans.* New York: Charles Scribner's Sons.

Green, Caitlin. 'King Arthur, the Arctic and Arcturus.' In *The Heroic Age: A Journal of Early Medieval Northwestern Europe* 15 (October 2012).

Green, H. S. 1975. 'Sudanese Radiocarbon Chronology: A Provisional List.' *Nyame Akuma* 6: 10-24.

Guerber, Helene A. 1985. *The Norsemen.* London: Bracken.

-----. 2006. *Myths of the Norsemen.* New York: Barnes and Noble.

Gurney, O. R. 1976. *Some Aspects of Hittite Religion.* Oxford: Oxford University Press.

Güterbock, H. G. 1964. 'Religion und Jultus der Hethiter.' In *Neuere Hethiterforschung.* G. Walser, ed. *Historia Einzelschriften* 7.

-----. 1965. 'A votive Sword with Old Assyrian Inscription.' In *Studies in Honour of Benno Landsberger on his 75th Birthday, April 21, 1965.* Chicago, pp. 197-198.

Haas, V., and G. Wilhelm. 1974. *Hurritische und luwische Riten aus Kizzuwatna*. In *Alter Orient und Altes Testament, Sonderreiche* 3. Neukirchen.

Hall, John Whitney. 1970. *Japan: from prehistory to modern times*. New York: Dell Publishing Company.

Hard, Robin. 1997. *Apollodorus: The Library of Greek Mythology*. New York: Oxford University Press.

Haynes, Sybille. 2000. *Etruscan Civilization: A Cultural History*. Los Angeles: J. Paul Getty Museum.

Heaney, Seamus, trans. 2001. *Beowulf: A New Verse Translation*. New York: W. W. Norton & Company.

Hedeager, Lotte. 1992. *Iron-Age Societies: From Tribe to State in Northern Europe, 500 B.C. to A.D. 700*. John Hines, trans. Oxford and Cambridge, MA; Blackwell.

Henderson, Arthur E. 1966. *Saint Paul's Cathedral: Then and Now*. London: S.P.C.K.

Herodotus. 1972. *The Histories*. Auberu de Sélincourt, trans. New York: Penguin.

Herzfeld, Ernst. 1947. *Zoroaster and His World*. Princeton University Press.

Hinnells, John R. 1975. 'Reflections on the bull-slaying scene.' *Mithraic Studies* 2:303-304.

Hreinsson, Viðar, et al. 1997. *The Complete Sagas of Icelanders Including 49 Tales*, Volumes 3 and 5. Reykjavík, Iceland: Leifur Eiríksson.

Jha, D. A. 1998. *Ancient India in Historical Outline*. New Delhi: Manohar.

Johannesson, Kurt. 1978. *Saxo Grammaticus, Komposition och världsbild i* Gesta Danorum. Stockholm: Almquist and Wiksell.

Jung, Emma, and Marie-Louise von Franz. 1986. *The Grail Legend*. Andrea Dykes, trans. London: Coventure and Boston: Sigo.

Kak, Subhash. 2006. 'Art and Cosmology in India.' *Patanjali Lecture* given at Center for Indic Studies, University of Massachusetts, Dartmouth, May 5, 2006. http://www.ece.lsu. edu/kak/ArtCosmologyDartmouth.pdf, Accessed 12/17/23.

Kao, Chü-hsün. 1960. 'The Ching Ly Shen Shrines of Hun Sword Worship in Hsiung Nu Religion.' *Central Asiatic Journal* 5(3):221-232.

Kershaw, Kris. 2000. *The One-eyed God: Odin and the (Indo-) Germanic Männerbünde.* Journal of Indo-European Studies Monograph No. 36. Washington, D.C.: Institute for the Study of Man.

Kibler, William W. Kibler. 1981. Chrétien de Troyes, *Lancelot or, The Knight of the Cart* (Le Chevalier de la Charrette). New York and London: Garland.

Kosambi, D. D. 1963. 'The Beginning of the Iron Age in India.' *Journal of Economic and Social History of the Orient* 6(3):309-18.

Krupp, E. C. 1978. 'Observatories of the Gods and Other Astronomical Fantasies'. In *In Search of Ancient Astronomers.* E. C. Krupp, ed. NY: Doubleday, pp. 241-278.

-----. 1983. *Echoes of the Ancient Skies.* New York: Harper and Row.

Lacy, Norris J., ed. 1993. *Lancelot-Grail: The Old French Arthurian Vulgate and Post-Vulgate in Translation.* Volume 2. New York and London: Garland.

Lacy, Norris, et al. 1986. *The Arthurian Encyclopedia.* New York and Garland.

Lambert, Nicole. 1971. 'Les Industries sur cuivre dans l'Ouest Saharien.' *W. Afr. J. Archaeol.* 1:9-21.

-----. 1973. 'Objets en cuivre et néolithique de Mauretanie occidentale.' *Actes Vie Congr. Panafr. Préhist. Dakar, 1967.* Paris, pp. 159-74.

Lawson, E. Thomas. 1985. *Religions of Africa: Traditions in Transformation*. New York: HarperSanFrancisco.

Lévi-Strauss, Claude. 1966. *The Savage Mind*. Chicago: University of Chicago Press.

Levy, G. R. 1953. *The Sword from the Rock*. London: Faber and Faber.

Lhote, H. 1966. 'La route des chars de guerre libyens Tripoli-Gao.' *Archéologie* 9:28-35.

Lincoln, Bruce. 1981. *Priests, Warriors and Cattle*. California: University of California.

Littleton, C. Scott. 1970a. 'The "Kingship in Heaven" Theme.' In *Myth and Law Among the Indo-Europeans*. Jaan Puhvel, ed. Berkeley: University of California Press, 83-121.

-----. 1970b. 'Is the 'Kingship in Heaven' Theme Indo-European?' In *Indo-European and Indo-Europeans*. George Cardona, Henry M. Hoenigswald, and Alfred Senn, ed. Philadelphia: University of Pennsylvania Press, pp. 383-404.

-----. 1981. 'Susa-nö-wo Versus Ya-mata nö Woröti: An Indo-European Theme in Japanese Mythology.' *History of Religions* 20:269-280.

-----. 1982. 'From Swords in the Earth to the Sword in the Stone: A Possible Reflection of an Alano-Sarmatian Rite of Passage in the Arthurian Tradition.' In *Homage to Georges Dumézil*. Edgar C. Polomé, ed. Washington, DC: The Journal of Indo-European Studies Monograph No. 3:53-67.

-----. 1983. *The New Comparative Mythology: An Anthropological Assessment of the Theories of Georges Dumézil* (Third Edition). Berkeley: University of California Press.

-----. 1995. 'Yamato-takeru: An "Arthurian" Hero in Japanese Tradition.' *Asian Folklore Studies* 54:259-274.

-----. 2007. 'Theseus as an Indo-European Sword Hero, with an Excursus on Some Parallels between the Athenian Monster-Slayer and Beowulf.' Los Angeles, CA: Annual Meeting of the Western States Folklore Society.

-----. 2008. 'The Sword in the Tail: Susanō, Yamato-takeru, and the Embedded Sword Theme in Ancient Japan.' Davis, CA: Annual Meeting of the Western States Folklore Society.

-----. 2008. 'Theseus as an Indo-European Sword Hero, with and Excursus on Some Parallels Between the Athenian Monster-Slayer and Beowulf.' *The Heroic Age*. https://www.heroicage.org/issues/11/littleton.php. Accessed 12/12/2023.

Littleton, C. Scott, and Linda A. Malcor. 1985. 'Did the Alans Reach Ireland? A Study of the Scythian References in the Lébor Gabála Érenn.' In *Homage to Jaan Puhvel, Part II*. Edited by Edgar C. Polomé. Washington, D.C.: The Journal of Indo-European Studies Monographs 21:161-182.

-----. 2000. *From Scythia to Camelot: A Radical Reassessment of the Legends of King Arthur, the knights of the Round Table, and the Holy Grail*. New York and London: Garland.

-----. 2004. 'From Scythia to West Africa: Ogun and the Sword-in-the-Stone Legend.' Northridge, CA: Annual Meeting of the California Folklore Society.

-----. 2006. 'The Germanic Sword in the Tree: Parallel Development or Diffusion?' Presented at the Western States Folklore Society annual meeting at Berkeley, California, Friday, April 21, 2006.

Loomis, Roger Sherman, and Laura Hibbard Loomis. 1938. *Arthurian Legends in Medieval Art*. London: Oxford University Press; New York: Modern Language Association of America.

MacCulloch, J. A. 1911. *The Religion of the Ancient Celts*. London: Constable.

MacMillan, K. 2001. 'John Dee's "Brytanici Imperii Limites."' *The Huntington Library Quarterly* 64:151-9.

Macqueen, J. G. 1986. *The Hittites and Their Contemporaries in Asia Minor*. Revised edition. London: Thames and Hudson.

Maenchen-Helfen, Otto J. 1973. *The World of the Huns: Studies in Their History and Culture*. Berkeley, Los Angeles and London: UC Press.

Magno, Oliveira. 1952. *Umbanda e Ocultismo*. Rio de Janeiro: Editora Espiritualista.

Malcor, Linda A. and John Matthews. 2021. *Artorius: The Real King Arthur*. Stroud, Gloucester: Amberley Publishing.

Malory, Sir Thomas. 1969. *Le Morte d'Arthur*. John Matthews, ed. London: Cassell 2000.

Matthews, John, and Caitlin Matthews 2017. *The Complete King Arthur*. Rochester, VT. Inner Traditions.

Matthews, John and Maarten Haverkamp. 2024. *The Prophecies of Merlin: The First English Translation of the 15th-Century Text*. Rochester, VT. Inner Traditions.

Mattingly, H. and S. A. Handford, trans. 1970. Tacitus, *The Agricola and the Germania*. Harmondsworth, Middlesex and New York: Penguin.

Mauny, Raymond. 1947. 'Une route préhistorique à travers le Sahara.' *Bull. Inst. Franc. Afr. Noire* 9:341-57.

McMahon, Gregory. 1991. *The Hittite State Cult of the Tutelary Deities*. The Oriental Institute of the University of Chicago. Chicago: Assyriological Studies 25.

Mercier, P. 1954. 'The Fon of Dahomey' in *African Worlds*. D. Forde, ed. London: Oxford University Press for International African Institute, pp. 210-34.

Métraux, Alfred. 1959. *Voodoo in Haiti*. Hugo Charteris, trans. Second edition 1972 with introduction by Sidney W. Mintz. New York: Schocken.

Micha, Alexandre. 1948. 'L'épreuve de l'épée.' *Romania* o.s. 70:36-50.

Mierow, Charles Christopher, trans. 1915. *The Gothic History of Jordanes in English Version*. Princeton: Princeton University Press; London: Oxford University Press.

Milisauskas, Sarvnas. 1978. *European Prehistory*. New York: Academic Press.

Millar, Fergus. 1966. *The Roman Empire and its Neighbors*. New York: Delacorte.

Miller, Dean A. 2000. *The Epic Hero*. Baltimore: Johns Hopkins University Press.

Mills, Stella M. 1933. *The Saga of Hrolf Kraki*. Oxford: Blackwell.

Misevich, Philip. 2018. 'Atlantic Slavery and the Slave Trade: History and Historiography.' *Oxford Research Encyclopedia of African History*. Oxford: Oxford University Press.

Moiraghi, Mario. 2003. *L'engima di san Galgano*. Ancora.

Muhly, J. D., R. Maddin, T. Stech and E. Özgen. 1985. 'Iron in Anatolia and the Nature of the Hittite Iron Industry.' *Anatolian Studies* 35:67-84.

Murray, Kevin. 2017. *The Early Finn Cycle*. Four Courts Press, Dublin.

Neu, E. 1974. *Der Anitta-Text*. Otto Harrasowitz: Studien zu den Boğazköy-Texten, 18. Weisbaden.

Nyberg, Tore. 1966. *Religionen des Alten Iran*. Osnabrück: O. Zeller.

-----, ed. 2004. *Saxo and the Baltic Region: A Symposium*. Odense: University Press of South Denmark.

Ōbayashi, Taryo, and Atsuhiko Yoshida. 1981. 'Tsurugi no Kami; Tsurugi no Eiyu: Takemizauchi Shinwa no Hikaku Kenkyu.' *Sword Gods; Sword Heroes: Comparative Studies in the Mythology of Takemikazuchi*. Tokyo: Hosei Daigaku Shuppankyoku.

O'Flaherty, Wendy Doniger, trans. 1981. *The Rig Veda: An Anthology*. Great Britain: Richard Clay.

Otten, Heinrich. 1961. 'Eine Beschwörung der Unterirdischen aus Boğazköy.' *Zeitschrift für Assyriology* 54:114-57.

Pemberton, John III. 1977. 'A Cluster of Sacred Sumbols: Orişa Worship Among the Igbomina Yoruba of Ila-Qrangun.' *History of Religions* 17(1):1-28.

Perrin, Bernadotte. 1914. *Plutarch: Lives*. Volume 1: 'Theseus and Romulus, Lycurgus and Numa, Solon and Pulicola.' Loeb Classical Library. Bury St. Edmunds, Suffolk: St. Edmundsbury Press.

Phillips, Kyle. 2012. 'San Galgano: Of Swords and Stones.' https://iwronline.blogspot.com/2012/10/san-galgano-of-swords-and-stones.html. Accessed 12/12/2023.

Phillips, Patricia. 1980. *The Prehistory of Europe*. Bloomington: Indiana University Press.

Plutarch. 1974. *Plutarch's Lives*. Alan Wardman, trans. Berkeley: University of California Press.

Prakash, B. and V. Tripathi. 1986. 'Iron Technology in Ancient India.' In *Historical Metallurgy*, pp. 568-75.

Puhvel, Jaan. 1987. *Comparative Mythology*. Baltimore and London: Johns Hopkins.

Rey, H. A. 1997. *The Stars: A New Way To See Them*. Enlarged World-Wide Edition. Boston: Houghton Mifflin.

Ridgway, David and Francesca R. Ridgway. 1979. *Italy Before the Romans: The Iron-Age, Orientalizing, and Etruscan Periods*. London and New York: Academic Press.

Ridpath, Ian. 1994. *The Night Sky.* Philadelphia, PA: Running.

Robert, C. 1873. *De Apollodori Bibliotheca.* Berlin.

Rose, H. J. 1959. *A Handbook of Greek Mythology.* New York: E. P. Dutton.

Sassoon, Hamo. 1962. 'Grinding Grooves and Pits in Northern Nigeria.' *Man* 62:145.

Sayers, William. 2013. 'Extraordinary weapons, heroic ethics, and royal justice in early Irish literature.' *Preternature* 2(1):1–18.

Schutz, Herbert. 1983. *The Prehistory of Germanic Europe.* New Haven and London: Yale University Press.

Schaeffer, Bradley E. 2006. 'The Origin of Greek Constellations.' *Scientific American* November 2006, pp. 96-101.

Senior, Olive. *Encyclopedia of Jamaican Heritage.* University of Michigan: Twin Group Publishing.

Shaw, Thurstan. 1978. *Nigeria: Its Archaeology and Early History.* London: Thames and Hudson.

Shippey, Tom. 2001. 'Wicked Queens and Cousin Strategies in *Beowulf* and Elsewhere.' *The Heroic Age* 5. https://www.heroicage.org/issues/5/Shippey1.html. Accessed 12/12/2023.

Sims-Williams, Nicholas. 2002. *Indo-Iranian Languages and Peoples.* Proceedings of the British Academy 116. Oxford: Oxford University Press.

Sivananda, Sri Swami. 1958. *Parables of Sivananda.* Uttar Pradesh: Divine Trust Society.

Spenser, Edmund. 1763. *A View of the State of Ireland as it was in the Reign of Queen Elizabeth.* Dublin: Laurence Flynn.

Stowe, Lyman E. 1907. 'The Story of Jesus *is* an Astrological Allegory *for* the Sun passing through the Zodiac each Year.' In *Stowe's Bible Astrology: The Bible Founded on Astrology.* Kessinger Publishing: Whitefish, Montana, pp. 130-136.

Sturluson, Snorri. 1987. *Edda*. Anthony Faulkes, trans. London: Everyman Books.

Sulimirski, Tadeusz. 1970. *The Sarmatians*. New York: McGraw-Hill.

Sullivan, William. 1996. *The Secret of the Incas*. New York: Three Rivers Press.

Sykes, Mark. 1904. *Dar-ul-Islam: A Record of a Journey Through Ten of the Asiatic Provinces of Turkey*. London: Bickers and Son.

-----. 1915. *The Caliphs' Last Heritage: A Short History of the Turkish Empire*. London: Macmillan.

Taylor, E. G. R. 1956. 'A Letter Dated 1577 from Mercator to John Dee.' *Imago Mundi* 13:56-68.

Thapar, Romila. 1991. *India Tales*. New Delhi: Puffin.

Thompson, Stith, and Jonas Balys. 1958. *The Oral Tales of India*. Indiana University Publications, Folklore series, no. 10. Bloomington: Indiana University Press.

Todd, Malcolm. 1992. *The Early Germans*. Oxford and Cambridge, MA: Blackwell.

Tripolitis, Antonia. 2002. *Religions of the Hellenistic-Roman Age*. Wm. Eerdmans Publishing.

Trowbridge, Stephen van Rensselaer. 1909. 'The Alevis, or Deifiers of Ali.' *Harvard Theological Review* 2:340-353.

Turnville-Petre, E. O. G. 1964. *Myth and Religion of the North: The Religion of Ancient Scandinavia*. Westport, Connecticut: Greenwood.

Tuso, Joseph F., ed. 1975. *Beowulf: The Donaldson Translation, Backgrounds and Sources Criticism*. New York: W. W. Norton & Company.

Ulansey, David. 1989. *The Origins of the Mithraic Mysteries: Cosmology and Salvation in the Ancient World*. New York and Oxford: Oxford University Press.

Vamplew, Anton. 2006. *Simple Stargazing: A First-Time Skywatcher's Guide*. London: Harper Collins.

Van der Merwe, N. J. 1980. 'The Advent of Iron in Africa' in *The Coming of Iron*. T. A. Wertime and J. D. Muhly, ed. New Haven: Yale University Press, pp. 463-506.

Varner, Gary R. 2007 *The Sword and Dagger in Myth and Legend*. Raleigh, NC. OakChylde Books.

Vermaseren, M. J. 1963. *Mithras, the Secret God*. London: Chatto & Windus.

Von Sydow, C. W. 1965. 'Folktale Studies and Philology: Some Points of View.' In *The Study of Folklore*. Alan Dundes, ed. Englewood Cliffs, NJ: Prentice-Hall.

Walker, Henry J. 1995. *Theseus and Athens*. New York and Oxford: Oxford University Press.

Ward, Donald J., ed. and trans. 1981. *The German Legends of the Brothers Grimm*. Philadelphia: Institute for the Study of Human Issues. 2 vols.

Webster, Kenneth G. T., ed. and trans. 1951. Ulrich von Zatzikhoven, *Lanzelet*. Revised by R. S. Loomis. New York: Columbia University.

Wells, Peter S. 2001. *Beyond Celts, Germans and Scythians*. London: Duckworth.

Whatmough, Joshua. 1971. *The Foundations of Roman Italy*. New York: Haskell.

Wiggerman, F. A. M. 1999. 'Nergal A. Philologisch.' In *Reallexikon der Assyriologie*, pp. 215-223. De Guyter.

Williams, Denis. 1969. 'African Iron and the Classical World.' In *Africa in Classical Antiquity*. L. Thompson and J. Ferguson, ed. Ibadan, pp. 62-80.

-----. 1973. 'Art in Metal.' In *Sources of Yoruba History*. S. O. Biobaku, ed. Oxford: Clarendon, pp. 140-64.

-----. 1974. *Icon and Image*. New York: Hew York University Press.

Yaggy, L. W. and T. L. Haines. 1884. *Museum of Antiquity*. Madison: J. B. Furman & Co.

Zangger, Eberhard, E. C. Krupp, Serkan Demirel, and Rita Gautschy. 2021. 'Celestial Aspects of Hittite Religion, Part 2: Cosmic Symbolism at Yazılıkaya.' *Journal of Skyscape Archaeology* 7(1):57–94. https://doi.org/10.1558/jsa.17829. Accessed 12/12/2023.

INDEX

Also available from Amberley Publishing

ARTORIUS
THE REAL KING ARTHUR

LINDA A. MALCOR & JOHN MATTHEWS

Available from all good bookshops or to order direct
Please call **01453-847-800**
www.amberley-books.com

Also available from Amberley Publishing

THE BOOK OF
MERLIN

MAGIC, LEGEND AND HISTORY

JOHN MATTHEWS
NEW YORK TIMES BESTSELLING AUTHOR

Available from all good bookshops or to order direct
Please call **01453-847-800**
www.amberley-books.com